# Your Story is Your Power

*Learn to share stories that sell*

Anna Simpson

978-1-915502-39-1

© Anna Simpson 2023. All rights reserved.

All rights reserved. No part of this book may be reproduced by any mechanical, photographic or electronic process. This book is created to inspire and equip you to share your stories with your audience, elevating your influence, increasing your value and maximising your profits. This book is designed to help you shine in your power and share your gift with the world. No liability is assumed for damages that may result from the use of information contained within. Published by Orla Kelly Publishing.

www.anna-simpson.com

*"The world wants to buy the inner hero. Release your inner hero and equip your outer warrior, so you can share a story that engages the mind and compels behaviour."* - **Anna Simpson**

# Contents

Introduction .................................................................. vii

1. Why Stories? The Importance of Developing the
   Story Acumen ............................................................ 1

2. Integrating Hero's Journey Methodology ........................... 20

3. How to Craft a Story. What Do You Share? ....................... 44

4. How Do You Clarify and Articulate Your
   Unique Voice? ........................................................... 79

5. How Do You Articulate it so People Pay Attention? ........ 107

Choose the Right Future Path ............................................ 126

Resources and Support ..................................................... 130

# Introduction

I tried snorkelling for the first time in the Maldives. I didn't know it at the time, but the experience was about to change how I viewed the world, and how I approached my coaching business. Despite knowing nothing about diving or underwater creatures, my husband managed to coax me below the waves.

I kept smiling, extending my arms, trying to say hello to all those fishes circling around me. They all had their own different personalities. At least, I thought they did. Some of them would stick to their packs, preferring the value of the community; others were explorers venturing into the remote parts of the coral reef. Some were shy, while others were curious. There was one particular fish — pearly white with a few black spots, I named him Johny, who was following me around. He was as curious about me as I was about him.

All the fishes were absolutely glorious. Stunning in their unique beauty.

If I could, I would be squalling with joy, admiring the underworld paradise, but the mask and the breathing tube were in the way. I had a revered sense of awe and admiration for the creator of the earth. It reminded me that we are all part of the beauty of this universe. How often do we forget our own magnificence? It is during moments like this that we become conscious of who we really are.

What was so insightful for me was the fact that all those fishes didn't compete but complemented each other, perfectly coexisting in their diverse world. There was no comparison, no self-deprecation, no rivalry. There was harmony. A perfect flow.

How different would our world be if we were to complement rather than compete with others? What if we were to accept the idea that there is room for everybody if we dare to embrace and express who we are? If we dare to stand in our unique beauty and value confidently?

The best way to express who we are and our unique value is through stories. Stories are our differentiator. Stories are the tool to help us stand out. Stories are an excellent way to contribute and make a difference. That's what we are going to focus on in this book. How to use stories to make a bigger impact.

When you read this short story, what feelings did it produce? Were you able to see or imagine the picture of underwater magic? Perhaps, you were thinking of your next holiday destination. Or maybe it brought back some memories if you have visited the Maldives before?

That's the power of storytelling.

I am excited about your decision to invest your time in this book. This book is designed to reveal the secrets of powerful storytelling and equip you with the tools to help you improve your business outcomes by connecting with your audience and customers in a more profound way. By the time you've finished reading, you will know how to craft your story to amplify your connection, influence and profit.

The stories you tell are a powerful way to communicate your message and connect with your audience. They can help you to inspire and motivate, or they can make a lasting impression on the people you meet.

**In this book, you will learn how to:**

- Develop a compelling and memorable story that attracts your audience's attention in a way that leaves them wanting more.
- Use storytelling as an effective tool for creating connections and building relationships with potential customers.
- Identify the values at the core of your business or professional services practice and use those values to craft a simple narrative that resonates with your audience.
- Use storytelling techniques to transform your business results.

This book is your guide to the world of storytelling. It will help you discover the elements that make a good story, how stories are formed, and why some are more powerful than others. You will learn how to use these techniques to create your own compelling narratives, which can be used to build relationships with your audience, communicate ideas, or sell products or services.

When I started sharing my personal stories publicly to improve my English and make friends in a new country, I didn't realise how much the power of stories would shape my entire life. It was transformational. Not only was I able to connect with people's hearts and inspire them to dream bigger, but I also went through a process of self-discovery and gained a better understanding of myself, my identity, and what I stand for.

It was a hero's journey that allowed me to embrace and share my value with the world. Winning speaking contests and sharing stages with iconic figures like John Maxwell, Seth Godin, and Bruce Lipton was a natural consequence of discovering my message and sharing my stories.

*Create the Life You Dream About* was my first book, featuring my story from poverty in Ukraine to building a dream life in the

USA on my own. It created a breakthrough in my life and defined my business concept. I have also written "Elite Influencers of the Coaching Industry," featuring the hero's journey stories of the founding members of our Conscious Coaching Academy.

I teach my clients that their past is their biggest platform and that the key to unlocking and expressing their genius is by unpacking their story and their hero's journey. You have a message to share, even when you sell tangible products in your business. The world needs to hear your voice and be transformed by your message.

We all have a powerful story that has the potential to change other people's lives. The best part is that you can get paid for being yourself while transforming other people's lives.

This book is written to help you find clarity, meaning, and significance in your stories so that you can integrate them into your business and create a more impactful influence on your clients.

You will be introduced to strategies, tools, and tactics for developing a story acumen that can be used in marketing, emails, courses, and programs. Let's dive into the art and science of sharing stories effectively to connect with the right audience.

# 1
# Why Stories? The Importance of Developing the Story Acumen

*"The universe is made of stories, not of atoms."* - **Muriel Rukeyser**

I am a passionate believer that stories have the power to revolutionise lives and businesses. Why is story the most powerful tool to connect with people's hearts and compel them to take action? Why is mastering your message the most important requirement for success? Why does any transformation begin with an inspirational story?

The answer to all those questions is simple. If you want to rise above average and enjoy the freedom and fulfilment of your heart-centred business, you need to learn to tell a better story.

Your influence starts with the story you tell.

Here is why. For someone to change their destiny, they have to make a decision. For them to make a decision, they need to change their emotional state. The best way to change their emotional state is through a story.

We are wired for stories. Since ancient times people have been sharing stories to explain natural phenomena, understand the dynamics of relationships and find meaning of life. We think in a story form. We explain new concepts with stories to illustrate the meaning.

Since ancient times stories have been used in all areas to help us unravel the essence of the world and what it means to be human. They show us what's possible, expand our imagination and encourage us to become our best selves. Stories provide direct access to a fascinating realm of another person's mind, bringing the inspiration for our own transformation.

> *"I am writing my story so that others might see fragments of themselves."* - **Lena Waithe**

As a child, do you remember being transported to the magical worlds of fairy tales and learning from the hero's adventures? How they fought the villains, undertook challenging journeys? Perhaps you recall being gripped as those characters battled injustice and were inspired by the ways that good conquered evil?

We are hungry for stories. We've been conditioned to be since childhood, and it's actually who we are. We start paying attention when we hear an interesting story. Stories engage our minds, spark curiosity and show us what's possible. They open our imagination.

## Stories speak to us at a values level

When I bought my first MacBook laptop, I didn't know at the time that I'd unconsciously connected with the values the Apple brand stands for. As Steve Jobs would tell his biographer before his death: "The people who buy Apple products do think different. They are the creative spirits in this world, and they are out to change the world. We make tools for those kinds of people."

This wonderful statement explains why I love Apple so much. Apart from the beautiful aesthetics of the products and their ease of use, the inspiration behind them speaks to me at a profound level. The brand reflects my values.

But this statement also explains a lot about Apple's success and how it became one of the biggest companies in the world. It wasn't just Apple's products, although they are brilliant, that created such a sensation. Many other computer companies have similar talent and potential, but they haven't created the same influence. This is because other companies sell a product, whereas Apple influences our thinking, connecting with us at an identity level, and resonating with our values at a soul level. We all want to be significant, a part of something bigger; to commit to a higher cause, and to make a difference.

Steve Jobs's words created powerful resonance across the world and became one of the most compelling messages of all times because he masterfully melded a story, a great product and an inspirational promise. We admire and quote Steve Jobs' speeches. We are drawn to his genius, his vision and his mission.

If you are an Apple product lover like I am, you have experienced the power of connection through stories. Perhaps, you didn't consciously realise it was the story behind the brand that influenced your buying choice. But it played its part.

The power of well-crafted messages allows companies like Apple to charge premium prices, and empowering marketing stories allow companies to achieve iconic status.

Stories will allow you to magnify your influence and impact.

## People want genuine connection

Here is the truth. People are tired of hyped-up nonsense and pie-in-the-sky promises detached from reality. People are tired of charlatans attempting to pull the wool over their eyes. They are fed up with being exposed to manipulative marketing tactics. The information market these days is full of pretenders who are happy to hoodwink vulnerable audiences in the name of profit.

With so much noise, competition and misconception on the market, people's radar of scepticism and distrust is sky-high. People are developing information fatigue, being bombarded by pitches from all corners.

It is becoming increasingly difficult to stand out in a saturated market. Stepping above the noise these days isn't easy. Just getting noticed and getting your message heard is an art in itself.

However, the good news for you is — people crave genuine connection now more than ever. They want to believe that transformation is possible for them. They want the meaningful and personalised influence of authentic leaders to help them get unstuck. They desire to shift their consciousness in the name of a better life.

This is where the power of stories enters, offering an ethical way to influence and persuade.

Think about it, we buy from people we know, like and trust. What better way to express who you are and help people get to know, like and trust you? Personal stories help build relationships, trust and credibility.

People first have to buy into you before they buy from you. The best way to position your value, credibility and wisdom is through sharing your experiences of what you claim to be an expert in.

Stories are a great medium to allow your audience to experience the solution before trying it, as you will paint the picture of transformation *for* them. This will be talked about later in the book.

## Making an impact through stories

Stories allow you to make an impact, and not just from the results that your product or service offers.

What is the difference between impact and results? An impact is a step above. When you are able to articulate an impact for your audience (that profound value of your business that makes all the difference) in a way that will make your customer say, "Yes, that's exactly what I'm after. How can we work together?", you master the art and science of business success.

And that's where stories come to your aid.

Stories provide the context for your transformational statement. Context gives everything meaning, breathing life into your message.

I believe you can be whomever you want to be if you dare to step up and enter your power consciousness, and here is some context about me.

I was born and raised in a small, poor Ukrainian town, called Polonne. I was blessed to have loving and caring parents but unfortunate enough to experience the pain of poverty.

At times, our family didn't have enough money to buy food. Thankfully, we had a garden with vegetables and fruits, and we had chickens and turkeys. But yoghurts? Bananas? Chocolate bars? Those were luxury items for special occasions.

We had running water, but we had to run to a well for it.

We didn't have a bathroom, shower or toilet inside the house. Taking a bath was an entire rigmarole, which required multiple steps — going to the well, bringing water in buckets, heating it on the stove and mixing the hot and cold water in a tub and then using a cup to pour water and wash ourselves. That was the process.

When I came to America and lived in a home with a proper bathroom and a shower with hot running water all day long, I couldn't believe my joy. I was like a child on Christmas morning. How soon do we take for granted the small, simple things that make us so happy?

I knew all about the external effects of poverty — the physical challenges that make life difficult, and I was also only too familiar with the internal consequences of being poor — the feeling of being undeserving of all the great things others had.

But there was something within me that refused to accept an existence of poverty and scarcity. I knew there was more to life than my current circumstances, and that the world was a much bigger and better place and could offer so much more than what my small town could give. I could see that the world was small and large at the same time — so I started looking for a key to unlock the bigger world.

When I was twelve years old, I said to my mom, "Mom, when I grow up, I want to live in the USA."

Her response was, "Honey, don't be ridiculous. It's impossible. People like us don't go anywhere."

I knew she had the best intentions to protect her daughter from bitter disappointment. To a certain degree, my mom was right; it seemed an impossible dream for someone who didn't have two pennies to rub together. Someone who was mocked and humiliated by kids at school for wearing old shabby clothing. Yet again, the spirit inside of me refused to accept that "truth". And it started seeking its higher expression.

One thing I learned over the years is when people tell you that your dream is impossible, it means it is worth pursuing it.

I promised myself at that young age that I would do anything possible and reach beyond any limits to bring my dream to life. It wasn't easy. While my college mates were enjoying summer holiday breaks, I would go to Kyiv to work in restaurants.

I started working when I was eighteen. Thankfully, I had a friend in Kyiv who allowed me to stay in her studio apartment. Sleeping on the floor wasn't an issue for me, as I was able to save every penny from the waitressing job, apart from those spent on food and basic living expenses. I was on a mission. It took me three years to collect the thousands of dollars necessary to pay for my trip to America.

My commitment, hard work and determination paid off.

3rd of May 2010 was the first day of the rest of my life. I landed in JFK, New York. I'd arrived in the land of opportunities on my own. I'd brought to life my big and impossible dream despite the odds stacked against me and all those negative messages of "it can't be done".

I'd read in books that the streets in America were paved with gold. But let me tell you, when I came there, I realised two things. First, the streets were not paved with gold, but with concrete, litter and the occasional heap of dog poop. Second, I was supposed to pave the streets of my own life.

Although I was in the land of opportunities, none of those opportunities was handed to me.

On my own, barely speaking English, and without *any* Professional qualifications, my initial challenges of finding a job became the catalyst for my strengths.

Yet again, I learned — if you persist, you achieve what you want. In the space of a few weeks, I went from being jobless to having three jobs.

I first lived in a small studio shared with five other girls. Living like kittens in a box didn't concern me at all. I was in America, courageously pursuing my dreams. I wasn't shy of hard work either and for a while I kept three jobs simultaneously.

After five months of living and working in America, my visa was coming to an end. That's when an unscrupulous immigration attorney took advantage of my status as an immigrant: vulnerable, naive and somewhat trusting of "authority", I handed over all my savings — a hard-won deposit of $3000 … and the unethical bottom-feeder of a lawyer disappeared without a trace, leaving me almost bankrupt and standing on a cliff edge and facing deportation back to Ukraine.

He knew I wouldn't do anything with my US visa about to expire.

Alone and vulnerable with only $600 to my name, I had to start my life from scratch all over again, but in a different state. And it was here, Florida, that things changed for me, though at first everything looked much the same.

My life in Florida came with plenty of challenges too, but in time, it became far more settled. I spent eight happy years there before moving to the United Kingdom after marrying my English Prince Charming. And yes, just before the move, I secured my long-desired American citizenship (one of the proudest moments in my life).

Now, my husband and I run the Conscious Coaching Academy. Our company trains and accredits people to become iconic coaches, equipping them to bring the most transformational process known to mankind — coaching. While my husband provides the coaching training, I am passionate about helping people find clarity in their message, confidence in their voice and the ability to articulate their story, so they can powerfully position themselves on the marketplace, express their talents and monetise their abilities.

I am absolutely convinced there is no such thing as an impossible dream if you give yourself permission to step up into your power consciousness and play a much bigger game.

Our past does not define our future. I am grateful for all those hardships and difficulties because they've helped me become who I am today. They motivated me to strive for achievement. They've pushed me to embrace my power consciousness.

If a simple girl from a poor family in a small Ukrainian town could go on to seize her opportunity in the USA and in the UK, I believe anyone can bring their dreams to life.

I encourage you to expand the limits of what you believe is possible for you. You have an amazing story to your name that has the potential to inspire other people's lives.

## You have a story worth sharing

What is the primary objective of sharing stories?

To make a difference.

I have worked with many people on their stories and most of them would start our first conversation with, "I don't really have a great story to share." And after we go through the process of unpacking their hero's journey and extracting their unique genius, they say, "I didn't realise my story is so inspirational. I really like it."

It warms my heart when I receive emails and messages of gratitude from my clients sharing how adding stories to their business and marketing helped them bring more clients, secure more contracts and elevate their influence.

One of my beloved clients, Magda, was stuck emotionally and financially when we first started working together.

She couldn't identify or articulate her business concept. She just had big dreams, yet her personal limiting beliefs were clouding her ability to recognise and define the value she wanted to bring to the marketplace, by using her talents and passions. "Everything is possible, but nothing is happening. I am sick and tired of being stuck," she would tell me.

So we started working together on identifying her strengths and unpacking her hero's journey. Her life had revolved around dancing ever since she could remember. Born in Poland, she was participating in multiple ballroom dance championships in her own country. After winning or becoming a finalist in many contests, she came to the international arena. She'd created a name for herself in the dancing world.

Later she moved to the USA, got married and had a child, and she seemed to have lost her sparkle. Yet, her potential was seeking its higher expression.

We devoted our energy and efforts to refining her business strategy, honing her marketing message, and fusing her vibrant personality with it. In the process, she reconnected with her vivacious self, reigniting her genius for dancing. Her confidence flourished, and she got a new and more meaningful sense of direction.

Now, Magda is successfully running a Dance Training Centre in Florida. She doesn't only teach people to dance, but she arranges dancing cruises to exotic countries, enjoying a vibrant and thriving business that brings her joy and makes a difference in other people's lives.

It all started with rediscovering who she really was — her story — which brought clarity to her message, striking conviction in her about her capabilities.

If she could do it, I know you can, too. I've seen what gets results. This book and my programs will equip you with the right tools and strategies.

You don't need to have rags-to-riches, tragedy-to-salvation or cancer-survival stories to inspire others.

I have worked with so many people, and everyone has a powerful story. It is a matter of extracting the gold, polishing it and positioning it in the best possible light.

Although we all have an inspirational story within us, sometimes it just hides behind the "stuff" that needs to be removed.

Here is a little story to illustrate what I mean.

I was so excited to find a box of my husband's mom's jewellery (she passed away long before I met my husband). And I was even more thrilled when Christian (my husband) said to me, "My mom would be happy if her daughter-in-law wore her jewellery."

"You mean I can take them?" I squealed like a little girl who was getting the barbie doll she'd dreamed about all year.

To which my husband smiled and hugged me. "It would mean a lot to me as well if my wife wore my mom's jewellery."

A beautiful moment.

As you can imagine, it was more than just rings and earrings. There was a deeper meaning.

When I started trying on some of the rings, I found they would have to be adjusted for my fingers because they wouldn't fit properly.

Besides, the stones of one of my favourite rings were soiled by "stuff" that had built up over the years, and it was hiding its shine and beauty.

It had to be cleaned and polished.

It is the same when it comes to your message and stories.

In order for your message to shine brightly, attract people's attention and awaken their desire, you must know how to position the diamond in the best light.

The problem with many people who lack clarity is that the "diamonds" of their message are hidden behind the "stuff", which I call fluff. "Pie in the sky" kind of promises which just create noise without sharing anything of substance… or personal insecurities: "who am I for people to listen to me?"

If I were to listen to you define what you do, how coherent, confident, clear and uniquely pertinent would your promise be? How do you integrate your story with your business concept?

For most struggling business owners, it is confusing and woolly.

Now, if you want your message to not only create a positive and engaging reaction from your audience but also have people ask about how they can work with you, you must clean your message.

Just like with my late mother-in-law's ring, you must get rid of the "stuff" that obscures the diamonds or the core essence when it comes to your message.

You can do it yourself (which might take a long time, as it is very difficult to see a picture when you are the one in the frame) or you can have a mentor help you extract the diamonds of your story.

## Where do you share your story?

Developing a well-crafted story is the most lucrative skill in your business. Stories lend power to your words. There are many ways in your business you can use your story. The three primary ones are: marketing, sales and content development.

You can use stories to powerfully position yourself on the market, for example, in your About Me section on your website, your advertising narrative, an introduction to a podcast or a speech, or a "who am I and why should you care" section in your webinar. Using a story is an unbeatable tool to position credibility in your sales process whenever you communicate with your clients.

You can share your hero's journey story whenever it's relevant to your audience, such as in your signature programs, courses and speeches. People learn best through stories.

Michelle, one of my success clients, developed her signature program based on her own story. Having worked in various leadership roles as a registered nurse, she was let go from the company she had dedicated thirty years of committed service to. After several months of playing the role of 'Failed-Michelle', she made a choice to replace the word failure with a learning opportunity. That shift in consciousness allowed her to focus on realigning her skill set with her passion to pursue her purpose.

Success was no longer about the title, but about walking down the path best suited for her. She dared to step out of her comfort zone, and despite facing challenges and difficulties, landed on her feet. She SOARED to the new heights of her career. SOAR became the acronym of her unique methodology.

In her coaching business, she helps women in nursing and medical professions monetise their skillset, experience and passion in a fulfilling way, either navigating a path to promotion or choosing a new career or organisation.

With her SOAR framework, Michelle helps her clients create Success — using their skill sets in a way that is valued and highly paid. She does this by evaluating individual Skillsets, discovering Opportunities (that they are not even aware of) and stepping into the right Action and accountability, allowing her clients to enjoy the Results they want for their careers. She always says with a smile, "I love watching my clients soar, showing the world who they really are."

Andra is another client of mine, and a shining example of how a story can elevate your brand.

Andra Munro went to school for interior design. Experimenting with light to find creative solutions inspired her to create a truly original mark in the industry. Trying to find the right lighting at the beginning of each design project drove Andra to experiment with different materials and concepts.

In her creative curiosity, she asked herself, "What if I could create the elements of lighting in a unique way to refine human senses while reinforcing the experience in our interiors?"

She started exploring lighting in an artistic way. Mixing light with the porcelain material allowed her to create truly bespoke installations. There is a magical story of unfolding — taking functional lighting and turning it into a meaningful sculpture. Andra doesn't just sell porcelain light installations (which add a unique and luxurious look to interior design); she helps people create a sensual atmosphere in their homes to reconnect with their inner light.

In fact, she doesn't start a project before she clearly understands the story behind the concept — what her clients want to achieve with a particular lighting solution. Not only do Andra and her business have a story, but she is also willing to listen and recognise the importance of her clients' stories.

The inspirational story behind her brand came from an event that "rocked her world".

The day her husband was told by doctors that he had one year left to live was the darkest point. Instead of saying goodbye and sinking into a dark misery, Andra and her husband bought a new house and became determined to turn it into a true oasis with their unique design — making the most of whatever time was left.

Eighteen years later (at the time of writing this book), her husband is still alive and runs a successful business. They are both convinced their own oasis helped him survive.

The impact of the perfect atmosphere with the perfect light turned out to be way deeper than Andra could ever imagine. According to her, our interiors can alter our moods, emotions and feelings. She believes humanity thrives through its senses, evoking emotions — emotions which bring meaning and sensuality to life, connecting our external, observable experience with our subjective, inner world.

Andra's powerful story was an essential component in attracting high-end clients paying premium prices.

The potential of stories is truly infinite.

## Getting paid for being you

You have a great message to share. You have a story that has the potential to make a difference.

Everyone has a compelling message wrapped in their life story. Your story can inspire others to transform their life. You just need to learn to communicate it in a clear, persuasive and irresistible way.

Imagine being able to get paid for being you.

In other words, imagine creating a transformational impact on people who resonate with your unique voice and distinct message and pay you premium prices to help them with their problems. What would it feel like?

Here is a catch: it is not enough to just share a story. You need to know *how* to share a story that people would want to hear. And there is another level — learning how to get paid for being you.

Here is a story to show you what I mean.

Once upon a time, there was a young woman who had a great story to share with people — a story of overcoming and achieving what seemed impossible.

She came all the way from a small Ukrainian village and a poor family to the USA on her own, working hard as a waitress that paid her bills but emptied her soul, and she knew she was meant for more.

Deep down, she had a dream of becoming a motivational speaker and inspiring people with her message. She knew she was born for something significant, and her personal story of overcoming challenges from poverty to power was meant to empower so many people. But it wasn't easy.

It was more difficult than she could ever imagine. But did it have to be?

Share your story, "they" said.

Be authentic, "they" said.

Just go for it, "they" said.

Get this software, "they" said.

Use this strategy, "they" said.

She was doing it all — like a mad woman, running from pillar to post, waking up to tumbleweed and crickets.

Meanwhile, to lift her spirits, she devoured every self-help book, course and program she could get her hands on.

There were many different voices speaking in her head. She was bombarded with so much advice it defeated the object — she was more confused than ever! So many tactics and tools, creating overwhelm, a lack of clarity and frustration.

There was always something missing. She was spinning too many wheels, getting nowhere. With so many opportunities yet no real traction, all the unrewarded hard work and effort undermined any remaining traces of confidence and self-belief.

If bits and pieces don't fit, it's usually because our frames of reference are off.

When she finally figured out how to create a compelling vision and soul-aligned business which represented a true extension of who she really was, she realised she was doing it all wrong …

You have probably guessed that woman was me.

In that disheartening wilderness, it felt like there must be something wrong with me. If others can successfully do it using the same systems, why can't I?

The 'I'm not good enough' monster reared its ugly head over and over again. It never stopped questioning my belief, confidence and competence.

Until I figured out the methodology to transform my life and bring clarity to my business (I will elaborate on it in the second chapter on Hero's Journey). The answer was stories — something I had right in front of my nose all that time, but I just couldn't see it. Although I'd been sharing stories before, there wasn't clarity and cohesiveness between my marketing message, the audience's needs and my personal story.

In hindsight, I had all the pieces of the puzzle, but I just could not put them all together to create a beautiful picture. I didn't understand how the parts would merge together. I was looking for an easy fix instead of going through the journey of transformation.

The first step to mastery is clarity.

The process of identifying clarity in my voice was a hero's journey. Little did I know all those challenges and hurdles along the way were needed for me to define and articulate my voice and embrace my signature so I could have a meaningful and tangible impact on other people.

It is about what you share, how you share it and who is listening. All of this is unfolded through your hero's journey, which we will uncover in the next chapter.

### Summary points

- ❖ People are wired for stories. They start paying attention when they hear a good one.
- ❖ Stories are crucial because they can help you elevate your influence on the market, allowing your business and products to achieve iconic status.
- ❖ Through stories, you can have a genuine connection with your audience.
- ❖ Stories help build trust, relationships and credibility.
- ❖ Through the power of well-crafted stories, you can share the impact your product or service provides.
- ❖ You have a story worth sharing that can make a significant difference in other people's lives. Sometimes it takes a little bit of digging, polishing and positioning the diamond in the best possible light to create an impact.
- ❖ You can get paid to just be you. You just need to discover a compelling message wrapped in your story and clarify how it merges with the market need.

# 2
# Integrating Hero's Journey Methodology

*"The world wants to buy the inner hero. Release your inner hero and equip your outer warrior, so you can share a story that engages the mind and compels behaviour."* - **Anna Simpson**

Have you ever wondered why you love the movies you do? It's very likely the main character resonates deeply with you due to the way she responds to the call to adventure, how she shows up to the challenges, the initial vulnerability, the difficulty, the injustice and the way she deals with it all, rumbling with the falls, to become all she needs to be to prevail and conquer.

The character, his story and his struggles are so enthralling because they remind you of you and your own. It speaks to you because you know you're not alone on the journey. It inspires you to show up to the best of your ability.

The secret to success is revealed in almost every movie we see. It's not what the hero gets by achieving her goal, it is who she becomes in the process of rumbling with the falls. And that's why it speaks to us in such a deep and profound way. The hero's journey seeks to awaken us out of unconscious living.

What makes any story interesting is the conflict, which is at the heart of a hero's journey.

If there were no conflict, no struggle, the movie wouldn't resonate. It wouldn't compel us. The harder the conflict faced, the more glorious the triumph is.

It mirrors the great truth of life. If everything was easy, there would be no personal growth, and today, we'd be all we're ever going to be. That should be a very disturbing idea to any genuinely growth-orientated person.

What's more, you'd never appreciate your dream. Imagine being denied the appreciation of living your dream and the appreciation of yourself in creating it! Could there be a more damaging and devastating denial?

It's during the moments of struggle you have to remind yourself that it's not about the trophy; it is about who you become in the process.

> **The process of becoming a hero is more rewarding than the crowning glory she achieves by completing her mission. Think about it.**

You have to remind yourself during the inevitable tough times that those challenges happen not TO you, but FOR you. The hero in your life will never exist if the challenges and obstacles weren't there to overcome to create the hero in the first place.

Evaluating your hero's journey allows you to see how your past can become your greatest platform for growing your business.

Imagine how your level of impact will increase if your audience were to look at you as the hero who can show them the way to their promised land (you're a hero already, even if you don't consciously realise it).

People love hearing other people's stories of achievement because it helps them realise that they, too, can become successful.

*"We like to think of our champions and idols as superheroes who were born different from us. We don't like to think of them as relatively ordinary people who made themselves extraordinary."* **Carol Dweck**

You are the hero in your own movie called Your Life. You write the script. Your own hero's journey is the platform to inspire your audience to become the heroes in their life.

How would you describe the heroes of your own movie? Think of some dark times in your life that turned out to be the catalyst for your transformation. What happened that made you question everything, including yourself? What was the turning point that made you who you are today?

Write down your thoughts on your own hero's journey. What was the dark period that served as the catalyst for a better life? What profound insight did you gain from it? How can it serve other people?

## Becoming the Visionary Guide to your audience

There are four ways you can show up and position your value in the eyes of your audience.

The following graph illustrates where most people operate while sharing stories.

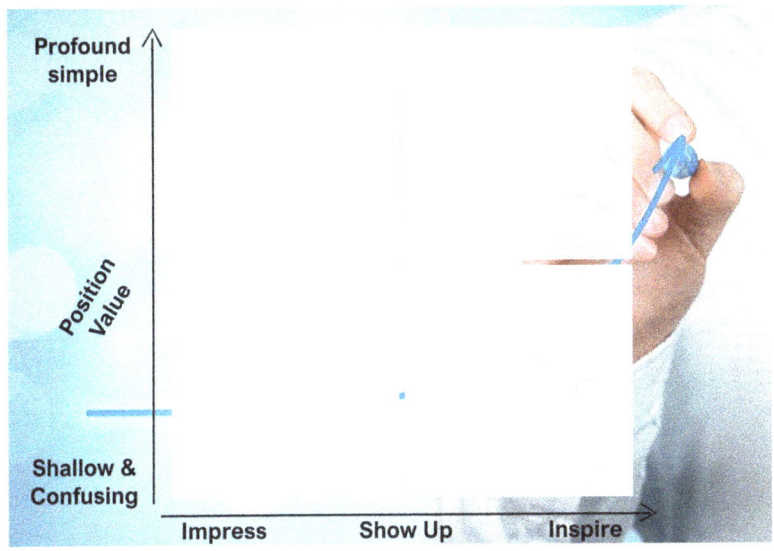

It is crucial to remember that the level of your impact depends on how you show up and share your value. Depending on how you show up and how you position your value, you either connect or repel your audience.

Many people share their stories to impress. If you show up to impress, it is about you and your ego. But when you show up to inspire, it is no longer about you, it is about your audience and how your story can serve them.

You also need to consider how you position your value. For most struggling business owners, the positioning of their value is shallow and confusing. However, when you learn how to position it in a profound yet simple way, everything changes.

Depending on how you show up and how you share your value, there are four dimensions you can occupy.

When your message is confusing and shallow, and you show up to impress, you occupy the space of what I call the copycat

— regurgitating someone else's ideas, quotes, phrases, and following templates because you haven't figured out what makes your offer different. Needless to say, the results will reflect that.

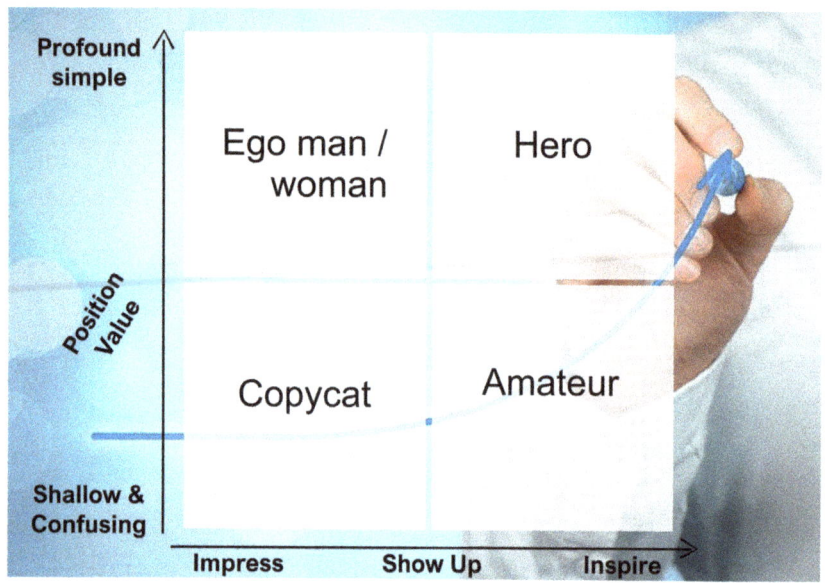

On the other side, you can have a profound value of your offer but if you come from the place of trying to impress people, you appear as an ego-driven person, which sends the message, "Look at me, I know my stuff, I have proven results. I am a big shot. But frankly, I don't care about you or your results, I am just here to share my proven secret methods." Unfortunately, the market nowadays is full of such experts who lack integrity.

The first shift occurs when you move your focus from yourself to your audience, from impressing to inspiring with your story.

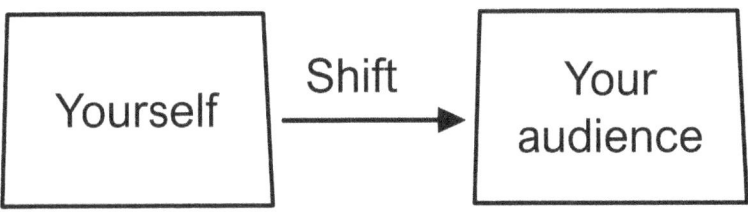

What happens when you come from a place of inspiration, but you haven't figured out how to articulate your profound value in a simple way? When you show up to inspire, but the positioning of your message is not clear, you occupy the space of being an amateur. What it means is you make awkward attempts at finding your unique voice and sharing your stories, but they are not defined or compelling. The conversation about your value is still shallow and confusing. There is no texture or depth to it.

In order to step out of the place of being an amateur, you have to share your story from the hero's journey framework.

In his book, The Hero with a Thousand Faces, Joseph Campbell, having analysed thousands of stories, has discovered a common pattern upon which all stories are built. According to the book, a hero ventures out of the ordinary world into the region of supernatural wonder, encounters and fights numerous forces to obtain a great victory and return home with a reward. Joseph Campbell describes seventeen stages divided into three categories the hero has to go through to get to victory. The hero has to go through the departure, initiation and return. The stages are:

1. The Call to Adventure
2. Refusal of the Call
3. Supernatural Aid
4. The Crossing of the First Threshold

5. Belly of the Whale (final separation from hero's known world and self)
6. The Road of Trials
7. The Meeting with the Goddess
8. Woman as the Temptress
9. Atonement with the Father
10. Apotheosis (the highest point of development of something)
11. The Ultimate Boon (the achievement of the goal or quest)
12. Refusal of the Return
13. The Magic Flight (the stage of the hero's journey in which the hero's return home is marked by a chase as the gods seek to regain the elixir that has been stolen from them.
14. Rescue from Without (aid from a powerful external benefactor to escape the realm of the supernatural and return home)
15. The Crossing of the Return Threshold
16. Master of the Two Worlds (the stage of the hero's journey in which the hero can move seamlessly between the two worlds, without destroying or compromising either)
17. Freedom to Live (the hero has found a balance between his internal and external worlds, and he no longer fears death)

In the context of personal storytelling, there are five stages of the hero's journey.

**Ordinary World.** Most stories begin with an ordinary world. What did it look like before everything changed?

**Call to Adventure** is the point when a hero is presented with a problem, a challenge or an adventure. She is motivated to exit her comfort zone into a special world of adventure. That's the place where she gets an "aha" moment to challenge the status quo. What was your call to adventure?

**Meeting the Enemies** is the stage where the hero, his character and determination are tested through obstacles, trials and hardships. The enemies could be visible barriers and inner fears, doubts and liming beliefs. What enemies did you face?

The next step is what I call **Fighting the Dragon**. This is part of the story that establishes the making of the hero. The hero usually hits bottom in confronting her greatest fear. It is a "life and death" battle with the hostile force that divides the story into before and after. By overcoming the most difficult ordeal, the hero gains a profound understanding of her identity, which allows her to get the reward. What was your biggest fear, and how did you overcome it?

**Getting the Reward** is the conclusion of the hero's journey when the hero obtains the treasure. What was the treasure you received by conquering the dragon? What was the knowledge and experience that brought you to a deeper understanding of your identity?

As you look at your story from the hero's journey framework, you can occupy the place of becoming the Hero to your audience. This is the level when you show up to inspire your audience and you share your profound value in a simple way. The ego is no longer involved. The hero comes from a place of lived wisdom. The hero has a genuine desire to share insightful lessons with others.

However, my goal for you is to take an even higher level than becoming the Hero in the eyes of your audience. You can become the Visionary Guide.

The Visionary Guide also leads from power and lived wisdom, being a transformational impact maker.

What is the difference between the Hero and the Visionary Guide?

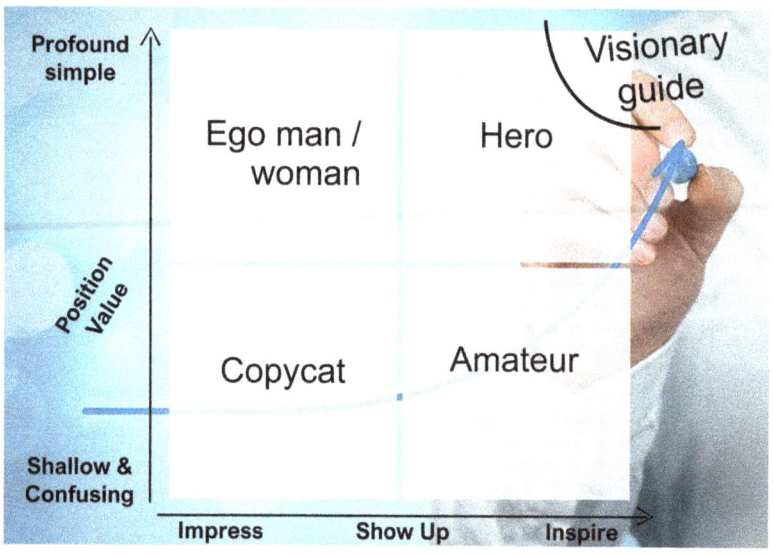

The moment you occupy the Visionary Guide, you move out of the hero space, making that space available to your audience, allowing your clients to become the hero.

With the power of your story, you show them what's possible; you create the path for them to become the hero; you invite them to join your world, so you can guide them to become the Hero of their own life.

You start with your audience and their needs, and you introduce yourself as a catalyst for helping them meet those needs.

The superpower of a Visionary Guide is to communicate profound ideas in a simple way anybody can understand and connect with — that's where the power of story comes in.

The moment you become the Visionary Guide, you become the guide the hero goes to.

Your influence on your audience becomes much more powerful when you look at your clients as heroes. But you first have to recognise your own hero's journey and how it has helped you get where you are today.

You can't become the Visionary Guide unless you own your own hero's journey.

## Examples of a hero's journey in business

As I briefly shared in the previous chapter, for a long time I was stuck trying to identify my message and create a sustainable coaching business.

Every programme I got my hands on talked about the importance of finding a niche and being very specific with the problems you solve for people.

You know when you try something, push hard at it, and it works?

That wasn't me. It normally takes much longer for my pennies to drop.

All those questions about identifying my market were not bringing clarity. "Your marketing proposition has to be tangible", every guru explained.

Tangible. How is coaching ever tangible? Transformation is like air — unseen, yet the substance of life. It remains out of view until it creates everything in the visible world.

I couldn't describe my value. Not in specifics. And not how the experts said it should be done.

The consequence? My message to the world was flaccid, flowery and wishy-washy — exactly what you get when you can't translate the power of transformation into material terms.

So, I went down the trial-and-error route. And as I'm not a girl who goes for half-measures, I made some substantial errors. Positioning myself as a motivational speaker, my target was the corporate world.

The first big lesson? Attempting to convince stakeholders you have what it takes to motivate teams of employees to increase performance is tough when you look like a fifteen-year-old schoolgirl.

"We don't hire motivational speakers. We hire people with expertise."

"Their loss," I'd say, my ego protecting me from yet another punch to an already bruised self-image.

Then, an epiphany. Sod these hard-to-please suits, I'll go down the relationship route. The world is full of single women looking for love. I knew; I was once one of them.

I was convinced I'd hit the gold. Here was a very specific problem, with a very specific outcome, and about as much emotional attachment in the client as you'll find in any sales situation.

Not only that, but I also had authority in the field. I could share the 'warts 'n' all' story of my hero's journey from the trenches of single life, getting abused and humiliated by the 'players', to finding Mr. Right and becoming a confident, loved, married woman.

The bright, new, shiny thing didn't last long. I soon realised it just didn't have meaning and heart for me — and I had enough about me to know if it didn't light me up and wasn't aligned with what I knew about my purpose, passion and vision, I'd never bring my best to life, and that, for me, just won't do.

And regardless, there was only so much I could talk about in terms of self-acceptance and how you must fall in love with yourself first before you can attract the right calibre of partner. I didn't have patience for the abundance of victim mentality and scarcity thinking I was constantly witnessing.

If I heard 'all great men are either gay or taken' one more time …

If you've ever had a conversation with a woman who thinks she's right and everything and everybody else is wrong, and it's 'not her problem that the world is so screwed up', you'll know exactly what I'm talking about.

Try coaching a woman that well-defended about her self-image and attitude!

No, this wasn't for me. I had little tolerance and patience with the women playing the blame game. They deserved better.

Then came the next "brainwave." Me as the "confidence expert". After all, confidence, or lack of, directly impacts people's lives. It resonated deeply with my own life experience, and I was happy with my message.

The problem? Too generic. Zero traction.

Boy, was I frustrated. It felt like this was my 'thing'… but my 'thing' just wasn't happening.

Being mentally stuck stinks. You've been there, I'm sure. It's not a healthy place to be and can descend, all too easily, into a downward spiral where fears are multiplied, and aspirations sacrificed on the great altar of doubt.

It happened on a beautiful, serene evening as I strolled down Hollywood beach in Florida, enjoying the light, salty breeze. Being in nature always provided a calming effect on me, giving me a bigger perspective. That evening, I had a heavy heart trying to find clarity around what I was doing wrong with my multiple trials in the business. I was bouncing from one failure to another without any hope of success. No matter how much I pretended, holding on to the straws of optimism and positive thinking, the reality was brutal.

I had no business results. I had no business, for that matter.

A few clients here and there did not even cover all the operational costs and investments into courses and programs.

I remember that moment of truth hitting me like a ton of bricks — I was a failure. My biggest fear: "I am not enough", was confirmed with big fat evidence staring in my face.

I dropped on my knees, feeling the hot tears streaming down my face. I surrendered to the painful moment and stayed there for a few minutes.

Did I come all the way from Ukraine to America to find out I was a failure? Was it who I really was? Did I come all this way for nothing? What was the point?

I was forced to go within to uncover my truth. Something I'd been preaching for a long time. And it was my turn to swallow my own pill. I knew all those negative voices were not speaking my truth, but they held me in an emotional trap.

No matter how hard it was, I chose to tune in with my higher self, and I realised all those failed attempts were like the scattered pieces I had to assemble into a puzzle to understand my own unique message. That moment of clarity was liberating. My vision was reignited with the newly clarified direction.

In the process of discovery, I found a method of clarifying a message and proposition that are in alignment with people's passion, purpose and identity. I was able to identify how unpacking a life story presents the clues of merging it with a massive market need.

Working with women who had the problem of finding clarity and confidence in their voice helped me distil the steps on how to get paid to be you. Those women were stuck and frustrated but had big dreams and ambitions to monetise their gifts. They lacked clarity which showed up in self-doubts, such as, "am I good enough?" and "who would want to listen to me?" They had exactly the same problems and aspirations as I did.

When I started coaching them, I discovered a pattern, a roadmap for finding clarity, which was directly linked to confidence.

So, everything I needed was within me, but I just had to figure out how to package it in a beautiful wrapping to awaken people's curiosity, interest and commitment.

My system is not just answering the question: who you want to serve, what their problem is, and what solutions you provide and wrap it up in a "hook-story-offer" model. It is a shallow approach. It lacks substance.

I go deeper. I help my clients change their mental state, awakening their creativity and facilitating the discovery of their own wisdom. I have developed the framework to translate who you are and what you have experienced into a compelling offer that gets traction on the marketplace.

How do you blend your hero's journey story with the massive market need? How do you express your ability in a way that attracts the right audience willing to pay you premium pricing to help with their problems?

In addition to this book, my signature programs beyond it will equip you to confidently position your expertise, amplifying your credibility through stories.

When you become confident in yourself, that confidence breeds clarity, and clarity leads to creativity. Confidence comes from knowing how to do it and actually doing it, which allows you to enter the state of flow and alignment.

Is it simple to get to the stage of being paid for being you? Yes, it is pretty simple. But I didn't say it was easy. If everything was easy, everybody would be skinny, rich and happy.

What makes the journey more enjoyable is the right guidance from a mentor, who can help you eliminate unnecessary struggle, and stop you from stabbing in the dark for solutions and allowing your negative inner voice to take charge.

I had to go through the trial-and-error route before clarity emerged.

All that time, I was sharing stories learning to connect with people, developing relationships with them and trying to convert them into my clients.

Although I didn't get the desired business results initially (read, make a lot of money), no effort was wasted. Going through the hero's journey allowed me to embrace my marketing message and offer. My hero's journey in business brought me clarity. And that is the reason why I do what I do.

I love helping my clients gain clarity and understanding of their hero's journey. I take people on a self-creation process to help them discover their unique voice, articulate their transformational message and equip them with the tools and resources to monetise their story, building a soul and heart-aligned business they love.

From overcoming major life difficulties of poverty in a Ukrainian village to building a dream life in the USA on my own and now running a global coaching business with my husband, my mission is to inspire, empower and equip people to shine in their power and get paid for who they are. Because it is possible.

Winston, one of the founding members in our Conscious Coaching Academy, walked the path of a hero's journey for eight years before he figured out how to create a successful insurance business. Despite hard work and doing the right thing for his clients, he kept failing initially.

Not being able to provide for his young family, living in a house he couldn't afford and seeing his university-educated wife work at fast-food restaurants to earn money for groceries was heart-wrenching. One day, he went to buy milk and gas with just ten dollars, swallowing the bitter realisation of the reality of things, he made himself a promise to become a man his wife and kids would be proud of.

The turning point for Winston was meeting his mentor, who introduced him to the power of crystal-clear vision. Winston calls it "my future me" vision, which in his words, changed his life. It became the pulling force in the most challenging moments. Every year he would go back to his vision and reflect on what had been accomplished and what needed to be adjusted.

After three failed attempts, he switched from life insurance to general insurance with the 4th company. Having worked hard for three more years, he was then able to buy that business and grow it exponentially, experiencing double-digit growth for the first four years. He managed to grow it from four to twenty-five employees, buy the second agency and purchase both buildings of his companies.

One Friday afternoon, he received an email with an offer to buy his business. All of a sudden, all the hard work, sacrifice and failures made it worthwhile. His success became tangible, giving him a fulfilling realisation: "I've made it".

Winston sold his business for a number that was ten times higher than the one he put on his vision ten years ago. He managed to find a way to get to his "future me" vision.

What inspired him to step into the coaching world is the feeling of obligation to share what he's learned during the struggling years of trying to crack the entrepreneurial code.

That's when he joined our Conscious Coaching Academy. Through elite coaching, he helps independent business owners create an effective growth model to navigate business transitions, grow profits and find the way to their future selves.

Stories like Winston's invigorate me, creating a profound meaning in what I do.

## Inspirational storytellers are made

Do you believe you could be a great storyteller? Do you believe you can be a transformational influencer?

Or do you buy into the "I am not good enough" voices?

When I was going to school in Ukraine, I was not one of the smartest or brightest students. I was a slow learner, who struggled with writing assignments.

The irony was that I really enjoyed Ukrainian language and literature classes. But they didn't like me.

I remember Miss Skoreiko, my Ukrainian teacher, gave us the assignment to read a novel and write an essay on it. I don't really remember what the novel was, but I remember putting so much effort into that writing assignment. I did my very best.

The next time, when the results were ready, Miss Skoreiko asked me, "Anna, did you read the story?"

"Of course, I read it. I really enjoyed it. Why?" I anxiously responded.

And she just said, "It doesn't show it. You can't really express yourself. You know, I don't think writing is for you."

She gave me the lowest grade in the class, just enough to pass.

I felt crushed.

When I moved to America, I was eager to learn English. So, I took a number of English writing and speaking classes at Broward Community College in South Florida. I loved studying, always doing my best. However, when it was time to submit the first written assignment, my stomach turned into knots.

I was a poor writer in my native language, let alone English. That was my reality. However, that didn't stop me from giving my best shot in composing an essay.

The next class, while awaiting my grade, I was close to having a panic attack. I couldn't breathe. I actually felt sick.

Mr Blanco, the professor of the English language, said to me, "Miss Anna, may I have your permission to show your essay as an example to my other students?"

My heart dropped to my feet. "Oh my God, it was so bad that he wants to show it as an example of how not to write," I thought.

The next moment, Professor Blanco handed me my paper with a big smile and said, "Excellent work!"

What?!! What does he mean by "excellent work"? Is he trying to mock me now? I looked at the paper, and I couldn't believe my own eyes. I got 100 out of 100.

That was a turning point for me and in my self-confidence. I am so grateful to Professor Blanco for giving me the green light to pursue my passions and for allowing me to develop my skills in writing.

Now, I am a published author. I've written and published two books already: *Create the Life You Dream About* and *Elite Influencers of the Coaching Industry*. And writing is one of the main activities in my business.

What that experience allowed me to understand is a great lesson. If you see people as they are, you only make them look worse. But if you see them as they could be, you help them become more than they could be — you help them live into their potential.

My Ukrainian teacher saw me as I was, and fair enough, I wasn't that good at writing in the beginning, even in my native language. But my American professor saw me as I could be. He saw the bigger picture for me, and he saw the bigger potential in me. And it inspired me to get reconnected with who I was meant to become.

What those two examples taught me is the importance of surrounding yourself with the people who lift you up, not tear you down, who build your confidence, not destroy it, who inspire you to grow and develop, not point at your mistakes and failures, and who encourage you to live into your full potential.

Professor Blanco was the catalyst that helped me to change the story I was telling myself about myself.

> **You are what you choose to believe you are. Choose the story that empowers you and don't be afraid to share it with others. The story you choose to tell yourself exerts a powerful influence over your ability to captivate others.**

Remember, great storytellers are not born; inspirational storytellers are made through relentless practice. You have a powerful story to share, you just have to extract it and articulate it in a compelling way.

Before we proceed further into the mechanics of writing a story, you must have an unbreakable belief that you can do it.

Your story is your calling card. Forget elevator pitches or sales techniques. Nothing beats the story. Your story is your power.

What is it you need to believe about your story to take it to the world that needs to hear it? Your belief about your ability to share stories is the stepping-stone in your ability to increase your income.

## Break free from your limiting beliefs

"Mais c'est impossible," my French teacher, Valerie said as we were discussing the book, *The Science of Getting Rich* by Wallace D. Wattles. Her main argument was — it is impossible to become rich without working hard. In her own words, she was not prepared to sacrifice the precious time of watching her kids grow up on "chasing the illusion of becoming rich."

"If I have to choose family or money, I will go for family," she concluded.

I'd hired Valerie to improve my French. As an avid reader, I'd picked my own method of learning the language — through books. So, I read books in French, and we discussed them during our lessons (which is how I learned English as well). And it is the best and most interesting way of learning a foreign language.

 As soon as I mentioned the topic for the discussion, the resistance was palpable in Valerie's entire demeanour. I knew it was going to be an interesting discussion.

During our session, I shared a few stories of a total life transformation to prove that the eternal principles in the book do work and that it is absolutely possible to achieve your dreams. I tried to refer to some of the famous names who live full lives, travel around the world and have work-life balance without having to choose family or money. I shared my own story and how I reinvented it in three different countries.

Valerie, however, didn't seem to hear any of my arguments.

When your belief in something is strong, you will not perceive any evidence contradicting that belief.

All she knew was that her father worked all the time, missing all the major events of his children growing up. "Yes, my dad had a successful career. But we don't have any memories of him other than being absent." That was her truth growing up — in order to reach success, you must work hard. That truth had turned into an unbreakable belief, affecting her entire life perception as an adult.

We don't see the world as it is. We see the world as we are. Oftentimes, our lenses of perception do not reflect the truth, or perhaps, not the truth in its entirety. Our beliefs about ourselves and how the world works often limit our possibilities.

While it might be true — plenty of successful people work hard (but when you are driven by passion, it doesn't feel like work). However, most people who work hard are broke. The sad reality is most people live from pay-check to pay-check with little to no savings.

My parents worked really hard all their life, but we were always broke. They were not aware that a totally different life could be possible for them if only they were to challenge their beliefs. There were plenty of other people in my native town whom I considered rich growing up. It is all about your level of awareness and what you believe is possible for you.

Through my life experience, I have learned that while your past conditions who you are, you can choose what is possible for you in the future. You can create yourself and your outcomes, without letting outside circumstances define what is possible for you.

Our discussion about money, achieving goals, and the philosophy of wealth was interesting, but the penny didn't drop for my French teacher. The new truth was too uncomfortable for her.

Did you know most people would rather be right than rich? The most mind-boggling fact about human psychology.

I encourage you to challenge your beliefs about what is possible for you. Especially when it comes to your storytelling ability. You have a lot of inspirational stories to share with others that could bring tangible market value. You have a unique voice to make a profound difference in other people's lives. You have the power to monetise your genius. But you must believe that your story and your voice matter.

Only if you challenge what you believe is possible for you can you achieve what seemed impossible before.

Henry Ford shared his wise words a long time ago, but they are still relevant today, "Whether you think you can or you think you can't — you are right."

There is a great story from an unknown author about how our beliefs keep us trapped. Quite literally.

There was a man who was passing the elephants. He suddenly stopped, confused by the fact that those huge creatures were held by only a small rope tied to their front leg. No chains, no cages. It was obvious that the elephants could, at any time, break away from the ropes they were tied to, but for some reason, they did not. The man saw a trainer nearby and asked why those beautiful, magnificent animals just stood there and made no attempt to get away.

"Well," he said, "when they are very young and much smaller, we use the same size of rope to tie them, and, at that age, it's enough to hold them. As they grow up, they are conditioned to believe they cannot break away. They believe the rope can still hold them, so they never try to break free."

The man was amazed. Those animals could break free at any time from their bonds, but because they believed they couldn't, they were struck right where they were.

A lot of people are held back by old, outdated beliefs that no longer serve them.

How many people do you know who have avoided trying something new because of a limiting belief? How many are held by someone else's limiting beliefs? The negative voice from the naysayers who give you all the reasons why you can't do something is based on their inner limitations or past failures.

The crucial part of success is mastering the inner game. You must recognise your value. Your story is your glory. What is your hero's journey story about?

You can have the best tools, strategies and tactics to build a successful business, but if you don't believe you can write a persuasive copy of your story; if you don't believe your voice matters; if you don't believe in yourself — you won't win.

80% of success is a mental game. You are in charge of your life because you are in charge of your beliefs. Do you believe your story would feed the soul of other people?

## Summary points

- You are the hero in your own movie called Your Life.
- When sharing your hero's journey stories, you need to show up to inspire your audience and position the value of your business in a way that will resonate with your audience.
- Incorporate the five stages of the hero's journey in your stories. Ordinary world. Call to Adventure. Meeting the Enemies. Fighting the Dragon. Getting the reward.
- The hero has a genuine desire to share insightful lessons from a place of lived wisdom with others.
- Your influence becomes much more powerful when you look at your audience as heroes.
- Inspiring storytellers are made. You can choose to become one.
- Your belief in your ability to share stories is the stepping stone in your ability to increase your income.

# 3
# How to Craft a Story. What Do You Share?

*"Stories you read when you're the right age never quite leave you. You may forget who wrote them or what the story was called. Sometimes you'll forget precisely what happened, but if a story touches you it will stay with you, haunting the places in your mind that you rarely ever visit."* - **Neil Gaiman**

Sharing stories can help you figure out how to craft a message that sells, so you can position it in front of people who are hungry to buy from you.

Stories can be actual stories you tell about your life (your hero's journey path that we discussed in a previous chapter), your business, your client's success stories or anything that illustrates your point and the message you are sharing.

What is a story, after all? A story is the language of experience. It is what happens to someone who is trying to achieve a goal, which takes them along a challenging path.

What is the difference between a story and a message? Although many people use these terms interchangeably, they are not one and the same thing.

A story is "what happened". A message is "what is the meaning of what happened? Why does it matter?" A story is a container for your message.

Gaining clarity in your message is the key to speaking to your clients' hearts and wallets, and it is attainable through learning the framework of storytelling for influence. This will be covered in the next two chapters.

## Share your authentic self

In order to inspire and motivate others, you have to be vulnerable. You have to be willing to expose your authentic self. Often it is uncomfortable.

People don't want to hear about your successes until they know you understand their failures. By talking about your own failures and struggles, you make an emotional connection with an audience. You become accessible and relatable. Once you make an emotional connection with your audience, you can take them where you want them to go.

I was ashamed of my story of poverty in Ukraine. Besides, I was thinking, how could anyone in the USA (in the land of opportunities) relate to the hardships of a young girl from a Ukrainian village? But when I started openly sharing about some of the challenges, I was genuinely surprised at the reaction.

I shared stories about how I was hungry many times at school because my mom couldn't always prepare lunch boxes or give me some cash to buy lunch at school.

I shared stories about how I felt ashamed of wearing shabby old clothing and facing mockery from school peers.

I shared stories about the fact that we never had Christmas or birthday gifts.

And people in America resonated with those stories. I guess, no matter where we come from, the language of pain is universal. After all, we are human beings with the same aspirations and the same struggles.

Although those stories were pulling some painful triggers, sharing them was therapeutic for me, and they were making a huge impact on my audience.

Inspiring influencers revel in their failures and embrace their struggles. Just like the pressure gives the diamond, the pearl and the grape their value, great storytellers turn their struggle into strength, conflict into confidence, and tension into triumph.

What is it that you could start sharing more openly to help inspire others?

There is a good reason why humans are hardwired to share stories and to enjoy listening to them. We need to. Stories not only help us survive; they help us on a personal level to make sense of the negative events all of us inevitably experience. Turning negative events into insightful lessons allows us to create a springboard for new beginnings. It is crucial to our survival, well-being and happiness. Behind every hero, there is a story of struggle and sacrifice, a story of dreams dashed, and dreams found.

We love hearing inspirational success stories of others, but when is it going be your turn to be an inspiration to others?

Imagine what it would be like to inspire others with your story.

Imagine what it would be like to ignite a spark in other people by just sharing who you are. You don't have to go through near-death experiences or starve as a child to empower others. Often there is more power in small but meaningful events. Just give yourself permission to share your power with the world.

You don't need to go on a missionary trip to Africa to share a powerful story on the value of giving.

You don't need to survive a terminal disease to express insight into the resilience of the human spirit.

You don't need to go bankrupt and lose millions in your business and then create even more success to show what's possible.

> **Often life-defining moments are quiet. They happen when no-one is looking. If there's one thing I've learned it's that what we feel is immaterial in our own lives is often tangibly invaluable to the lives of others. It brings them awareness without paying the price of their experience.**

## Where do you begin?

There are three types of personal stories you can and should share: origin story, turning point story, and "identity" story (an event that defined who you are).

Depending on where you want to focus your attention, each type has the hero's journey as the foundation to share the story of transformation.

Share your story of transformation and make it relevant to your audience.

Stories about transformation have moments of revelation or realisation that divides life into before and after.

I often share my story of transformation about an epiphany I once had in a restaurant.

I was working at a restaurant, hating my job. Nothing against the waitressing job, but it wasn't for me. One night, carrying trays heaped with dirty plates, I thought this was not the American dream I was hoping for. *I am here in the USA, in the land of opportunities, working just as hard as I was in Ukraine, in the land of no opportunities.*

I looked at Rosemary, my co-worker, who was born in America, but she was working just as hard as me. And she had nothing, the same as me.

And then, it hit me. It is not about being around opportunities. It is about being able to see and seize those opportunities. And that requires courage and capability, so you can step up, dare greatly and play a much bigger game. I remembered the expression I heard from one of my mentors. "You have to jump, building your wings on the way down." It spoke to me at a soul level. It was time for me to step up.

I didn't want to end up like Rosemary and remain as a server. I had a dream of becoming a person of influence. So, that night, I stepped up from being a server in a restaurant to become a server of the world. Nothing outwardly changed, but everything inwardly was transformed. My vision became clear, and my courage and capability became mine to own.

I got my coaching certification after, and I started speaking publicly, sharing my story from poverty to opportunities anywhere they would have me. I was jumping, building my wings on the way down.

I was calling myself a motivational speaker, speaking at different networking groups, Toastmasters (speaking clubs) and social gatherings. I was getting compliments, awards and winning speaking contests, but I wasn't getting paid. I was too generic in my message, and deep inside, I didn't believe I was good enough for people to pay for my expertise.

That was until I figured out what I needed to change in my approach to making money, using my coaching and speaking skills. The change didn't happen overnight, but in the process of becoming, I have figured out the clarity and confidence blueprint to allow me to share the story that people would want to hear and pay money for. That breakthrough mechanism gave me the clarity and confidence to build the business I love while transforming other people's lives.

The reason most people struggle in business is because they don't have clarity and confidence in their message. They are unconsciously driven by poverty consciousness. They don't believe they are good enough to impact other people's lives, and they don't have the right framework to create and share clear and compelling marketing messages.

So through my work, I help people discover their unique and confident voice, reflecting their expertise and genius, and blend it with the big need in the marketplace, so that they can become transformational influencers by doing what they love and getting paid for it.

Now, your turn. What is your story of transformation? And how is it relevant to your audience?

## What is the structure of the story?

To make a difference with your story, it must have a proper structure.

Depending on the purpose of your content, the layout of a story is pretty straightforward. It contains three indisputable elements: opening, main body and conclusion.

In the opening, you want to capture people's attention, and it must be engaging and interesting. A big promise. A powerful statement. A thought-provoking question. But it has to be compelling, which means you need to avoid a lengthy introduction. You are not writing a "war and peace" narrative. Start with a chase or a punch in the face, like in a James Bond movie. Get straight to the point.

For example, in my story about my ex-boyfriend, whom I thought was the love of my life but who turned out to be just a cruel womaniser, I open it with the words, "I was twenty-four when I thought my life was finished."

It automatically captures attention, making the audience wonder what could have happened to a young woman who had her whole future ahead of her, to think her life was over. The purpose of an opening is to intrigue an audience to want to find out more.

The main body covers your argument. This is where you create an emotional experience by telling a story with challenges, turning points and invaluable lessons.

Going back to my boyfriend story, I share some of the poignant details of a heartbreaking moment when he kicked me out of his apartment, saying I was just like every other woman, and he didn't want to deal with my drama. I was crushed and broken to pieces. He was a multimillionaire. I was a waitress. And it wasn't meant to be.

Then I continue to share the emotional experience through some actual events. Such as, having to carry trays with dirty plates in the diner I worked at after flashy dates at upscale restaurants was brutal enough. But him saying I was worthless was like a dagger stabbed straight into my heart.

Worse yet, I believed him. The tragedy was I fell in love with the guy, not his money. Only on the fourth date, I discovered he was a Russian oligarch. He was smart, with a great sense of humour and a brilliant thinker. In a way, he was a role model to me on how to reach success. And I have to admit, his sky-scraping success was the cherry on the cake. But the Cinderella tale was not my story.

The shift from living an existence of poverty in Ukraine to tasting life in limos and private jets really messed up my brain.

After a pity party consisting of sobbing on the bathroom floor, not showering for a week and wanting to end my life, I had a clear realisation — no one was there to rescue me. I had to hit rock bottom to recognise that I was the hero I was waiting for, and I could rescue myself. That heartbreak was the catalyst for my transformation from a victim to a confident woman.

In a story, a conclusion is the summary of your argument, which you want to make impactful, memorable and relevant to your audience. So, in the conclusion of my boyfriend story, I share an insight that served as a stepping stone to gaining strength in my self-worth, encouraging my audience to stop waiting for the outside rescuers and become the heroes of their own lives. My message is — we have the power to solve our problems, no matter how harsh they seem to be.

The elements of the story that bring the structure to life are character, conflict, struggle and resolution.

*"Listeners are rarely hooked if they don't sense some compelling challenge in the beginning. They won't stay engaged if they are not excited by the struggle in the middle. And they won't remember or act on the story unless they feel galvanised by its final resolution."*
**- M Guber**

## Share a story, make a point

It is crucial to remember that any time you share a story, you have to make a point. That's what creates the essence of a story. A story without a point is like a body without a heart. A point without a story is like a heart without a body.

While the structure aspect is quite easy, the essence part could be a stumbling block for many people.

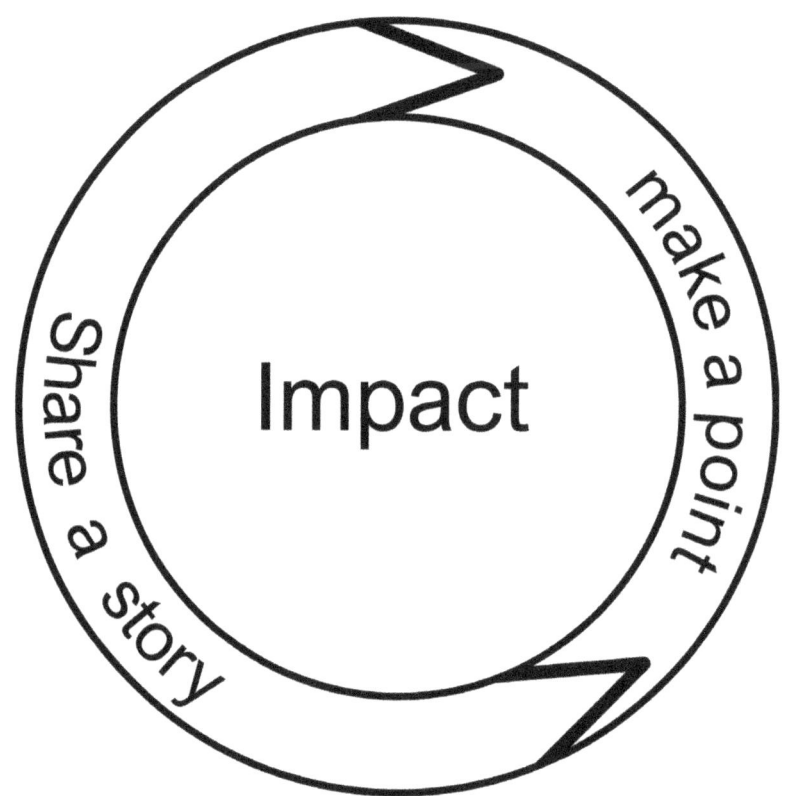

You have to learn how to extract a point from your story that will hit home and resonate with your audience.

What hooks us in a story is not beautiful language, carefully selected metaphors, or interesting characters. What hooks us is something that keeps the whole story together.

> **The big message — overcoming challenges and becoming the hero of our own life. It gives us the gift of unpacking the essence of what it means to be human.**

How do you make your story worth listening to?

How do you pick the most interesting and relevant details to captivate your audience?

How do you draw an incontestable lesson to bring an *aha* moment to your audience?

That takes a commitment to refine your thinking, clarify your ideas and intentionally apply the right framework (which this book gives you).

Steve Jobs was right when he said, "Simple can be harder than complex. You have to work hard to get your thinking clean to make it simple. But it's worth it in the end because once you get there, you can move mountains."

Start with your audience and their needs and introduce yourself as a catalyst for helping them meet those needs, and a story will instantly begin to unfold.

At the end of the day, it is not enough to have something to say, you must be able to say something that people would want to hear.

## Identify what you are trying to say

Here is the problem: most people create noise with the copy of their stories. It can be passionate noise, but in the end, it is still noise. Some sound too melodramatic or flowery, while others are dry and matter of fact. Some are polished, while others are jargon and cliche-filled. The bottom line is poorly written messages don't connect and don't convert.

I am speaking from experience.

Here is a little story to illustrate what I mean.

I was working with my mentor, preparing for an important speech for an international conference.

I was putting a lot of energy and effort into the preparation, crafting my story and spending multiple hours on making it interesting, juicy and insightful… I knew it had to be world-class because I would share that story in front of 4000+ people.

The process of preparation involved recording myself, listening to it, reflecting, changing, and tweaking the message. I did it a dozen times before submitting my first video to my speaker mentor for a critique.

I was sure my story was great, as it was my absolute best. However, his feedback took me by surprise.

He simply said, "Very good, Anna, but what are you trying to say?"

"What?! What does he mean, 'What am I trying to say'? Did he even watch the video?" I couldn't believe what I was hearing.

I was livid. My enormous efforts were not appreciated. It was as if my powerful and inspirational message had landed on deaf ears.

But then I calmed down and asked myself, "What exactly am I trying to say? What do I want my audience to walk away with?"

Funny enough, I wasn't clear on the answer myself.

The problem is, we have so much to say when it comes to those life-changing moments with so many variables and moving parts. How do you pick the right story-worthy details to make your message effective, relevant and sticky?

You cannot just share the facts of what happened and expect it to make a good story. The heart of a story only beats because of what those events mean to you.

*"Books say: she did this because. Life says: she did this. Books are where things are explained to you; life is where things aren't." -* **Julian Barnes**

I was determined to figure out how to craft my story to make it work. I would persist, working with my mentor and listening to his critique and remarks.

It is so important to have people in your life that can point at areas that you cannot see yourself.

Anyhow, I would go back to that story again and again, only to hear, "Well done, Anna, but I know you could do better." Or "Great job, Anna, but if you want to really connect with people, you need to take it to the next level."

During that process, he would ask me some questions that would elevate my thinking and my awareness.

When I got to present my story on a big stage in front of more than 4000 people, I was so glad I put hundreds of hours of preparation into a five-minute talk.

Do you know that pleasant internal feeling you get when you are doing a good job and connecting with people?

That was my reward.

Your efforts always pay off.

This experience made me realise how important it is to have a mentor. It is difficult to read a label from inside the bottle. You need someone who can see the bigger picture for you to expand your awareness. Sometimes, you can be too close to your own ideas to be able to pull out the pure gold that will make all the difference for your audience. A mentor will help you clarify your story and refine your message, which will compel your audience.

I am passionate about helping people extract their stories and messages. So I'm extending my hand of help to you. If you are ready to take your story to the next level, respond to any of my emails, or send me an email to anna@anna-simpson.com with the subject line 'help', so we can talk.

## Clarity in your definition formula

Working on a story, you must be able to answer three questions with clarity.

1. What are you trying to say (what story do you want to share, and what insights will it bring to your audience)?
2. How certain are you in your message? Do you believe in its value?
3. What is this story meant to tell your audience? How does it relate to them?

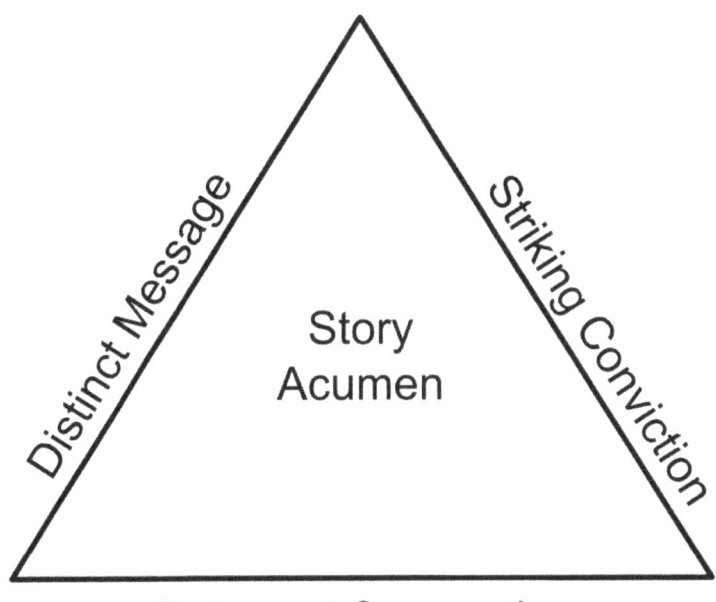

By clarifying these questions, you will master the art of storytelling or what I call, Story Acumen, encompassing a distinct message, striking conviction, and a relevant connection to your audience. As a result, you will be able to compel people's behaviour.

I am going to explain each point of the story acumen with a story illustration.

## Distinct message or 7 $/hour job and its lessons

Let's talk about the importance of a distinct message.

I used to stand under a scorching hot South Florida sun for about 7-8 hours a day.

Being a hostess in a restaurant in Miami Beach was one of the toughest jobs I've ever had. Yes, there was an umbrella, but it was still unbearable.

It wasn't just physically and emotionally draining; I was constantly full of fear and worry.

There was so much pressure on me from the management and the entire staff.

You see, my job wasn't just meeting and greeting customers. My job was to persuade the strolling tourists to dine in the restaurant.

The restaurant was located on Ocean Drive, right on the beach, with a beautiful ocean view. The location was perfect, and it was always busy with people.

The only problem was, there were about forty other restaurants on that 1.3-mile street. The competition was horrendous.

All those poor tourists were constantly bombarded by special offers at every step. By the time they reached the restaurant I worked at, they were quite annoyed at such aggressive advertising.

I did my best, using all my charm, positive energy, and big smile. But there is only so much you can do to get people's attention within seconds.

The worst part was, I was making $7 an hour, which would make about $200 – $250 a week. For Miami, it was impossible to survive.

I didn't last more than two months there.

What I learned from that experience is that the problem was not the competition. The problem was "being like everyone else."

That restaurant was just like everyone else: American/Italian cuisine, 2-for-1 drinks, and dinner specials (mainly seafood and steaks).

The management and marketing team didn't do anything to make that restaurant stand out by even simple changes or tweaks.

I was blaming myself for doing a bad job, but the problem wasn't me or my selling and communication skills. There were just way too many similar restaurants.

The competition in the marketplace is fierce. So, unless you have a distinct message, it is hard to stand out.

For any business, it is so easy to get lost in the crowd, becoming invisible. Even if you offer incredible value with your products and services.

I see it all the time.

It is very difficult to sell coaching or info products if all you do is what everyone else does.

The biggest problem I see with new coaches is that their offer doesn't differ from millions of others.

They are too generic with all-encompassing promises: live into your potential, achieve your dreams, create happiness, have financial freedom…

All of that is good, but what does it mean? Whom does it speak to? What does it communicate?

The promise and the message aren't sticky and compelling enough to elicit a commitment to action.

Your job is not just to inspire people and make them feel good with your stories. Your job is to inspire them to take action and work with you. If you want to be successful, of course. You must set yourself apart by sharing your distinct message.

## Striking conviction — and don't apologise for your experience

The second element of story acumen is striking conviction. What does it mean?

Let me illustrate it with a story.

"It was a wonderful speech. Congratulations. But you must be careful using strong language towards a certain profession. It might be offensive towards some people."

That was one of the comments I received after participating in a speaking competition and getting first place.

I was polite to that person, smiling and thanking him for the compliments. I didn't comment on his feedback.

The story I shared in my speech was about my experience working as a waitress. And I said that I hated that job because deep inside, I believed I was destined for more, which started an exciting journey of growth and self-leadership.

Apparently, "Mr. I'll give you constructive feedback", took my comment about my experience of waitressing as a derogatory judgement towards the profession itself.

It wasn't my intent. I remember saying, "Nothing against the waitressing job, but it wasn't for me. I was destined for more."

He took it as an offensive comment. Perhaps, he was a waiter himself, or one of his friends or loved ones was a waiter. Perhaps, I pulled some emotional triggers in him because he was stuck in life.

I am not sure what his reasoning was, but I am certain that my conscience was clear. I didn't attack anybody personally.

Reflecting on it in my car while driving back home made me realise that I should not apologise for my experience. I can use strong language if I choose to. It is my life and my perception of it, and I am free to speak openly about it.

If you can't openly and honestly speak your truth, you can't claim to be a thought leader.

## Your Story is Your Power

If you cannot openly and explicitly share your experience and your take on things, you don't have what it takes to be a successful storyteller. Or a successful entrepreneur, for that matter.

Some people are like wall flowers. They are fragile in their belief system, and they are easily offended. Moreover, they constantly look to be offended.

No matter what you say and how you behave, there will always be criticism, masking either jealousy or personal insecurities.

We see what we want to see. We interpret things based on our own frameworks and patterns, which are not always accurate.

My speech wasn't even about the waitressing profession, it was about the courage to follow your dreams.

But that person wanted to focus on the "negative" reference towards a restaurant job. He totally missed the point about thinking and dreaming bigger.

Your message must radiate striking conviction.

In my experience, life favours those courageous enough to be their true selves, even if it means "offending" someone.

Some people will never resonate with your opinions and journey. Some people just can't take your success.

As long as you don't infringe on other people's rights or freedoms, you are free to do and say what you please.

If it offends somebody, it is on them, not on you.

Be bold. Be courageous. Be you. The world needs you!

In the influencer industry, you cannot afford to be a vanilla ice-cream type of person. First of all, you can't please all people. And second, the simple vanilla flavour is boring. It makes you invisible and lost among thousands of other vanilla-flavoured people.

Solution?

Add some sprinkles. Or maybe, chocolate or coconut shavings. Perhaps, roasted salted nuts …

My point is you don't have to change who you are at the core. I personally love vanilla ice cream. But I like to make it more exciting, add more flavour, and make it more delicious.

Don't worry about some people not liking roasted salted nuts or chocolate. There will be plenty of other people who will love your particular favour.

Just don't be afraid to add some…

## Relevant connection, or do you sell air?

The story acumen triangle is incomplete without a relevant connection to your audience.

So, what exactly do you do? Is a simple question that most people have a hard time explaining with clarity and persuasion. Even some of the established businesses selling tangible products have a hard time talking about their product in a simple, clear and persuasive way. Most coaches don't know how to package their service in a way people would want to buy.

I was one of them.

When I discovered that I wanted to help people in some shape or form, inspiring them with my stories, I wasn't clear on what exactly that would look like.

"What is it exactly that you do?" asked my uncle in Ukraine.

After a fifteen-minute explanation, he looked at me suspiciously and concluded, "So, you sell air."

Oh, dear …

I mean, we are talking about Ukraine, where information marketing is a relatively new concept, and it is unheard of in small villages. But I still wasn't able to explain it in such a way that would make him go, "I see. I get it."

Technically, yes, I do sell air that allows people I work with to breathe freely in life without hassle, worry and fears.

I am passionate about helping people to get oxygen in the lungs of their businesses and life. But that definition was too poetic and abstract. That's why my uncle wasn't able to understand the meaning of the work I do.

As I continued walking down my hero's journey, I was able to conjure up a more tangible explanation. "I help people to define their message, which reflects their passion, vision and purpose and has a significant market value."

Through coaching 1:1 clients, I was going through a fascinating process of seamless self-discovery, helping people gain clarity on their vision and purpose and creating an action plan to achieve it.

Selling coaching and information products is like trying to sell air. Although coaching is the fastest-growing industry, it is still new.

It is an easy and hard sell at the same time.

Here is why it is hard.

**Coaching** is not a necessity. It is not on the top of the shopping list for most people.

**Coaching** is not covered by medical insurance.

While every person can absolutely enhance their life with coaching, it is not seen this way yet.

Therefore, coaching is not something a person needs. They must want it before they buy it.

**Coaching** is a luxury.

It is kind of like an expensive perfume. You don't really need it to survive, but if you love the smell and it makes you feel good, you find the money. It is the same with coaching and information services.

Coaching becomes easy to sell if you know how to position it in the right way.

People don't want to be sold to, but they are looking for value that can enhance their lives.

You have to master the art of connecting with your audience. Only then can you persuade your customers that your product or service will absolutely change their lives.

You must be clear on what you offer and who will benefit from it.

> **When you make your audience feel seen, heard and understood, selling, which is really a value exchange, becomes a natural consequence.**

When you have a distinct message to differentiate your service, a striking conviction to courageously share your voice, and a relevant connection to resonate with the right audience, you have a great foundation to share powerful stories.

## Unpacking clarity, value, and persuasion

In the context of the coaching industry, when people want to make a business out of it, the first question they ask is, "How do I get clients and make money?"

It is a fair question because your business is just a hobby without paying clients. However, it is a shallow conversation.

If you imagine an iceberg, everything above the water level is shallow, and everything below the water level is deep. The tip of an iceberg that perks up right above the water level is tangible and visible. But it is shallow. A shallow approach to building a successful business elicits shallow thinking. And the greatest form of shallow thinking is asking the question, "How do I get more clients and make more money?" And most people stay at a shallow level, perpetually struggling to get their business off the ground.

The truth about an iceberg is that no matter how much wind blows at the tip of an iceberg, it always moves in the direction of the base.

All the majesty is at the base, below the water level. So it is your choice — do you want to stay shallow or go deep?

If you choose to go deeper, there are three critical pillars your story must be built upon in order to elevate your impact, connect with people's hearts and compel their behaviour. These outcomes are clarity, value and persuasion.

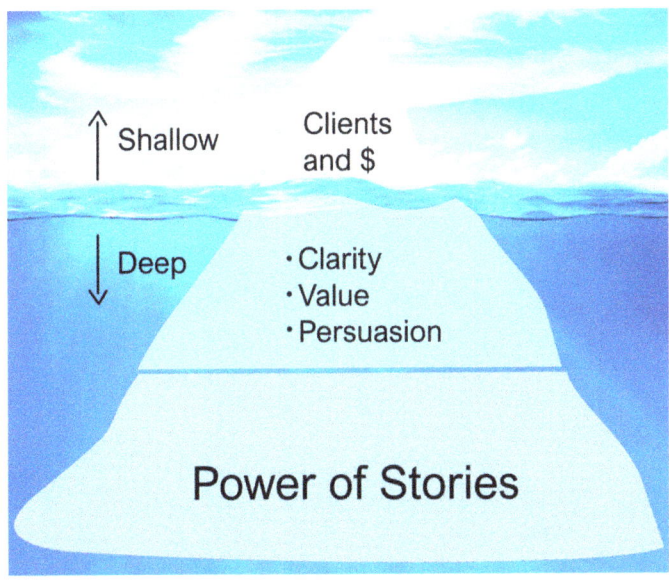

**Clarity** addresses the question, "How clearly does your story paint a picture of transformation?"

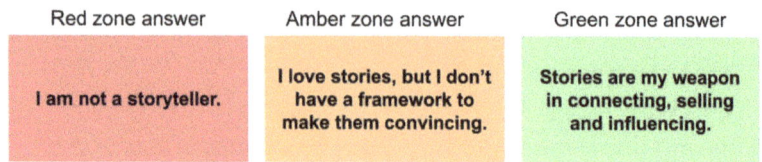

Which category do you fall into?

All mastery begins with clarity. Clarity is the foundation of a powerful and persuasive story.

How clear are you about where you are going and where you are taking people?

What is the direction of your life's work?

To master this element, you must integrate the hero's journey framework of your story of overcoming in a way that will resonate with your audience. You must unpack what, where, why and how questions, setting the context to deliver your message.

What is the true meaning of what you do? What happened in your life (your hero's journey) that transformed the way you look at life and people? Where were you before you were able to shift your consciousness, altering the course of your outcomes? What courageous steps did you take? What did you discover about yourself? Why should others care about your realisations? How are your discoveries relevant to your audience?

Think of your story as a path of transformation that will inspire your audience.

Until you establish what exactly it is that you are offering and what specific results it will bring to people, you will struggle to get clients.

To get crystal clarity in your thinking, you must go through the following steps:

*Cluelessness.* This is the stage when you have so much to share, and you are not quite sure what will be attention-worthy. It is usually the first step in the process of discovery.

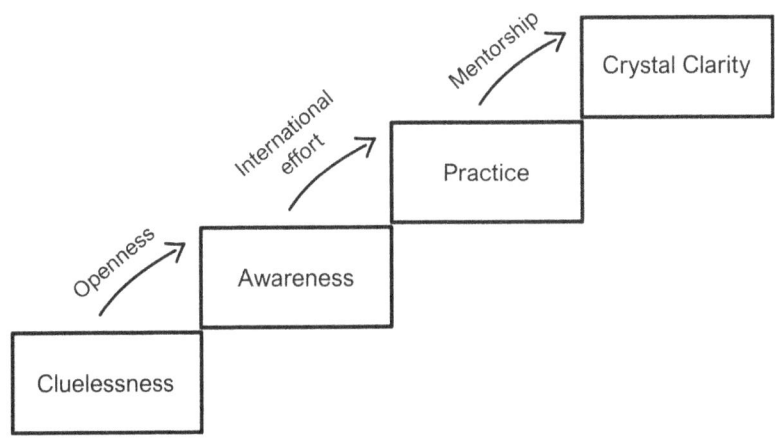

*Awareness.* If you are open to expanding your awareness in narrowing down your thinking, your consciousness shifts, and you are able to be and see more.

When you become more aware, you start putting in your intentional effort, *practising* your craft and becoming better at sharing stories.

When you seek mentorship to evaluate your practice, you achieve *crystal clarity.*

Mentorship with a strong focus on coaching (asking curiosity-based searching questions) brings you the qualitative input you need that's outside of your own consciousness. This is because you need the consciousness of somebody else to be able to bring to you what you can't see, as without this, you will only be looking at your story through your own eyes. When you share your story, you then bring your story to other people's consciousness.

People will surrender to your stories with ease when you learn the craft of sharing stories of possibility so that they can see that possibility for themselves.

The second pillar is **Value.** It addresses the question, "How clearly can you express the tangible and reveal the intangible value your product brings through a story?"

| Red zone answer | Amber zone answer | Green zone answer |
| --- | --- | --- |
| I'm not sure what tangible and intangible outcome means when it comes to my service. I just help people. | I use generalities around performance improvement that don't always relate to my clients' specific needs. | I communicate the outcomes specifically. |

Which category do you fall into?

"What value do you bring?" is such a simple question, yet most people struggle to clearly explain it.

The reason for it is that language is abstract, while life is not abstract. It's very specific. Teachers educate pupils on animals, battles and books. Doctors repair problems with kidneys, hearts and backs. Companies create planes, computers and cars. Even the most abstract business strategy shows up in tangible and specific steps of human beings.

When it comes to coaching, the ultimate goal is transformation. The problem is transformation could mean a plethora of different outcomes. For some people, it could mean shedding those annoying ten pounds; for others, it is finding a soulmate who will accept them for who they are; and for some, it is quitting that detestable job and doing what they love.

What does your offer help people achieve? Who are those people, and what are they struggling with? What keeps them awake at 3 am? What do they think about when they blow candles on their birthday cake? What does transformation mean in your world? Can you clearly articulate it?

If you try to speak to everybody, you end up speaking to nobody.

When you clarify who exactly you want to speak to and what transformation means to them, use a powerful principle of storytelling — show, not tell. It will allow you to share the tangible and intangible value your product or service brings.

Imagine trying to teach a four-year-old the abstract concept of addition and subtraction: 3+3-2=4. A child will be confused. Imagine showing a child three apples, adding another three, then taking away two to illustrate the concept of addition and subtraction. It is a totally different explanation which invites understanding. Show, not tell. When people understand you, you can influence them.

Any abstract concept demands a concrete foundation. Trying to explain abstract principles (transformation, freedom, abundance, etc.) without a concrete foundation (what exactly transformation, freedom and abundance translate into in a tangible reality) is exactly the same as trying to build a house by starting with the roof in the air.

You need both — abstract and concrete, or intangible and tangible value to be effective. Your money comes from the value you create.

**Persuasion** addresses the question, "How clearly can you articulate your promise to awaken people's desire for your offer?"

| Red zone answer | Amber zone answer | Green zone answer |
|---|---|---|
| I sound awkward and waffle. | I am pretty clear on my promise, but it is not unique or persuasive. | I have a proven process that makes my message convincing. |

Which category do you fall into?

- Do you really believe your offer is valuable and it will massively enhance your customers' life?
- Do you believe it is your responsibility to share your gift with the world?
- Can you make your audience feel confident you are their best chance?

If it is not a resounding yes to these three questions, you need to work on persuading yourself first.

Here are a few practical steps on how to get in a green zone, where you exude confidence and persuasion.

- Reflect on the positive feedback you have received from those who have benefited from your knowledge. Recognise the potential impact your message can have on people's lives and visualise the positive outcomes it can bring.
- Gather evidence that supports the significance of your message. Seek testimonials, success stories, and examples of how your expertise has made a difference. If you are just starting, imagine the profound impact you will be able to bring to your audience (remember, what you think you become). Surround yourself with like-minded individuals who share your passion and vision, as their encouragement and support can further bolster your confidence.

❖ Finally, embrace continuous growth and improvement. Stay updated with the latest developments in your field, invest in your own education and skills, and strive to consistently deliver exceptional value to your audience.

Trust in your abilities and let your passion guide you.

When you are persuaded yourself, it becomes easier to ethically persuade others to work with you, because you can clearly position the value of what you do.

Your job is to make them feel that what you have will change their life. Make them feel the pain of not making a choice and amplify the aspiration for what's on the other side of the struggle.

When a person is about to buy something, they are asking themselves three questions:

1. Does this work?
2. Can this work for me?
3. Can I trust the person who is selling this?

By "this", I mean the solution to the problem or the path to their aspiration.

Your job is to aggravate the pain of no change and amplify their desire. You persuade them to work with you when they clearly understand why working with you is their best chance to create a lasting transformation.

*"Persuasion is not about how bright or smooth or forceful you are. It is about the other party convincing themselves that the solution they want is their own idea."* - **Chris Voss**

How will you change their world in the context of what you do?

The story you tell gives your audience certainty. The story does a heavy lifting in your ability to clearly explain the solution and show how it will work. The story paints a picture of transformation. The story builds your credibility.

When people feel certain about you, they feel confident with your solution.

## Define your story thesis

When you start working on any story, you must create a story thesis.

What is your one big idea? You must clarify that one big idea in a single sentence.

According to dictionary.com a thesis statement is a short statement, usually one sentence, that summarises the main point or claim of an essay, research paper, etc., and is developed, supported, and explained in the text by means of examples and evidence.

A story thesis is a transformation statement, which is the bridge to close the gap between pain and pleasure for your customer. Define pain and pleasure in a clear, succinct and compelling way. Your transformational statement will become a solid foundation to build your story upon.

For example, our Conscious Coaching Academy provides accredited training creating elite influencers in the coaching industry, so they can lead with impact and integrity to transform lives, build legacies and grow 6-and-7-figure businesses.

The problem we saw was that most people in the market who call themselves coaches don't have proper qualifications and training, which undermines their confidence (their belief to make a difference) and competence (the ability to facilitate that difference). Hence most are stuck, frustrated and struggle to get by.

The mission of the Conscious Coaching Academy, as the definitive centre of excellence, is to disrupt the coaching industry of pretenders and wannabes by providing world-class training to equip elite influencers for far more influence, impact and income.

And the ultimate purpose of our work is to raise the consciousness of humanity.

It is a big and bold claim, but we have tangible evidence from the stories of our clients to support this claim and demonstrate our value on the marketplace.

What is your transformational statement? What difference are you called to bring to this world?

Once you clarify the foundation of your message or your big promise, you can put any story around it to communicate a more profound impact on your audience.

## An investable story behind your offer or the rubbish box story

The moment I realised the power of stories as a difference maker in marketing was at the Miami Art Basil Show. I admire creative expressions in different forms and shapes. During that exposition, I had a plethora of emotions ranging from fascination, admiration and inspiration to surprise, laughter and even confusion and shock. It was a true testament to the human imagination.

What particularly caught my attention was a wooden box standing in front of the exhibited pictures. The box contained all sorts of things: unfinished canvas, wrapping paper, scotch tape, carton boxes, plastic bags, picture frames, and even used coffee cups and beer bottles.

My first thought was — somebody left this rubbish box in a hurry. Perhaps, it was the container of the canvases. But it had to be taken away immediately; it obstructed the view of the pictures. So, with my willingness to help, I decided to inform the art agent about that little problem. Maybe (as often happens with creative people), he was way too absorbed with the art collection he was representing, and that minor detail skipped his attention.

He saw me hovering around the box and came up to me. I could literally see the spark light up in his eyes.

"Excuse me," I said, "what is this rubbish box doing here?"

He smiled and responded, "It is not a rubbish box, it is an art installation."

"An art *what*?" I was confused.

"This structure is an article of art. It is the symbol of the life of an artist behind the scenes," he explained, with clear notes of passion. "The rubbish box (as you named it) is a metaphor representing rejections, errors, failures, disappointments and fears …" He went on to say, "When an artist makes it, people see the glamorous side of things; they don't think about the hard path to the top, but it exists, and it is represented in this box."

"Food for thought," I thought but didn't say anything.

"Do you sell it?" I was curious.

To my big surprise, that art installation was an item for sale. And the cost of the rubbish box (as I appropriately named it) was just $25 000. The art agent said there were a few galleries interested in acquiring that piece of art, so the price might go up.

*You are kidding me*, I thought, speechless. I thanked the agent for such a passionate explanation of that "piece of art" and continued enjoying the celebration of human creativity.

But I couldn't stop thinking about that rubbish box. You can sell anything in this world, even trash, if you market it correctly. By marketing it correctly, I mean sharing an inspirational story behind your brand.

Driving home, a question occurred to me.

> **Don't all successful people have the rubbish box? The box of mistakes and failures, rejections, frustrations and enormous unrewarded efforts before they become successful? The invisible hard work and persistence are actually what create the essence of the hero journey stories.**

Most people are unwilling to put in energy and effort without seeing visible results immediately. It is not that they lack commitment; they choose not to be committed. We live in a society with immediate gratification expectations.

We refuse to exercise tenacity, persistence, and determination. We want the results now; we don't want to experience the rubbish box. The truth is if we can't handle the rubbish box, we can't enjoy the success box. Because the rubbish box comes before the success box.

## But I don't have interesting stories

Many people don't believe they have stories worth sharing. First of all, let me challenge that belief. I can guarantee you have interesting, insightful and inspirational stories. You just need to know how to find them.

Second, you must condition yourself to see stories around you. How do you do it?

Become the collector of stories. Everyday situations will give you a perfect opportunity to find insightful stories. Apart from your origin or personal stories, you can find great ideas for stories while you are having dinner in restaurants or enjoying your macchiato cappuccino in coffee shops.

Watch people's behaviour, listen to their conversations, learn to see things in a different way. Sometimes, what you see around you will bring up a great memory with story-worthy moments. Keep a journal of your collection of interesting observations. Pictures could be a great aid to help the memories stick. Cultivate mindfulness to be more present so you can see stories at every corner. Everyday scenes can present an excellent opportunity for an insightful story.

Like the one I witnessed at the airport. As we were walking towards our gate with my husband, I saw a lady walking on a moving escalator. Everything would be fine with that picture except for the fact that the escalator was moving in one direction, and the woman was going in the opposite direction. I was confused. I looked twice, but that's exactly what was happening. And the funny part of that situation was that the woman had no clue of what was going on around her. Clearly, she wasn't conscious of the fact that she was going in the wrong direction.

That's something you don't see every day, but actually, it is something you do see every day. How many people do you know who seem to be moving but they aren't going anywhere? Who seem to be busy but not productive, who seem to be involved in a lot of activities but not creating desired outcomes.

As I was reflecting, I realised that I was just like that woman at one point in my life. When I first came to America, I was working in a restaurant, and I hated my job. And every day, I would come to work, and I would be serving people, cleaning tables, doing the same things over and over again. I was busy, but I wasn't going anywhere. Just like that woman on the escalator, I was moving, yet

I was stuck. But I was hoping for better results and better life, not realising how insane it was. As A. Einstein said, "Doing the same thing over and over again, expecting a different result, is a sign of insanity."

This is a simple observation with an insightful lesson.

You have a plethora of stories that you can use. You just need to find them.

## Summary points

- Differentiate a story from a message. A story is "what happened". A message is "what is the meaning of what happened?" A story is a container for your message.
- Make an emotional connection with your audience by sharing your authentic and vulnerable self.
- Share your story of transformation, making it relevant to your audience.
- Clearly identify what you are trying to say and why it matters.
- Story acumen consists of a distinct message, striking conviction and a relevant connection to your audience.
- Your story must have clarity — clearly paint a picture of transformation.
- Your story must express tangible and intangible value to your audience.
- Your story must clearly articulate the promise to awaken people's desire for your offer.
- Your story must convince your audience the solution they want is your product or service.
- Define your story thesis, which is your transformational statement, as the bridge to close the gap between pain and pleasure for your customer.
- You can sell anything if you market it correctly. By marketing it correctly, I mean sharing stories behind your brand.

# 4
# How Do You Clarify and Articulate Your Unique Voice?

*"Finding your voice is about having the confidence to know you matter so you can use your voice."* - **Cammi Granato**

Undoubtedly, you have heard the saying, "wolf in sheep's clothing"? The mainstream interpretation of that metaphor refers to a dangerous person pretending to be somebody they are not.

However, it is a shallow explanation. What is the true meaning of Aesop's little story? If you go deeper, you'll understand the message of the story: don't try to fit in. Be yourself. You are better off this way.

The first step in discovering your voice is to make a firm decision to be sincere and genuine. Be you. Everyone else is taken. Show up courageously in your truth.

The journey from a wannabe to a transformational influencer is paved by finding your unique voice. Your lived experience is powerful and has the potential to inspire others. Do not think small of yourself.

As we go through the techniques and tactics on how to articulate your unique voice, the foundational part that no one can teach you is realising that you have one.

If you don't believe you have something of value to share, no system or strategy will help you.

Finding your voice begins with owning your story.

Do you own your story? Do you pride yourself on how you showed up facing challenges that built your character?

## How do you own your story?

I remember when I was thirteen, I came to school in a new winter coat. Mom and Dad finally got me a new coat, which I was so excited about. The problem was — it had a few seasons of growth to it (money was always tight, so my parents couldn't afford to get me a new wardrobe each season).

As soon as I entered school, there stood Angela Dubrovsky, the most popular girl in my class, who was always dressed immaculately. She gave me the look as if I was some disgusting creature that needed to be squashed. I honestly would prefer to have been squashed at that moment.

My other classmates, as if following Angela's lead, started giggling, exchanging glances with each other. I knew they were judging my grotesque look — oversized coat, long, skinny legs, and worn-out winter shoes.

I hated my classmates with all the fibres of my being. However, I hated myself more. Why couldn't I be like them? Why were my peers better than me?

I was never accepted in my school circle. I couldn't fit there. On the street (where I lived), I couldn't fit in with other kids (despite my desperate attempts to become friends with them). I was pushed away from their circle.

You see, I wasn't a cool kid. I didn't have a bicycle, so I couldn't ride with them. For the first eleven years of my life, we didn't have TV, so I couldn't participate in discussions about movies, shows and programs. I was excluded. I didn't belong.

My mates thought I was weird, an outsider. Although I wanted to have friends, I preferred to be on my own, as there was no judgment, separation, talks behind my back or humiliation.

My poverty was excruciating. I was humiliated, embarrassed, and ashamed. The only explanation I could come up with was — I wasn't good enough. We were not good enough as a family.

That created a dark place of shame for me, where I felt worthless at an identity level. Sometimes I was able to suppress that inner voice of personal inadequacy with positive thinking, but somehow it would always find its way to shrink back and sabotage my success.

My pent-up emotions were creating my self-narrative. That negative inner narrative was my constant companion, even when I escaped that poverty and moved to the USA. It was always subconsciously controlling my decisions, actions and results.

I tried to disown the parts of my story that once made me ashamed to appear whole. I didn't realise my wholeness depended on the integration of all my experiences, including the ones that made me feel ashamed.

Whenever there was an obstacle, a challenge or a problem, I would take it personally, letting my "I am not good enough" inner monster rub her hands, saying, "See, I told you."

A constant battle raged between me versus ME, my negative inner story and my higher self.

Only when I started to own my personal story, did I begin to see its gift in my personal healing. It took courage to share the details of my childhood and youth, to appear vulnerable and emotionally transparent.

However, I was amazed to see my story resonate with an American audience. I never thought the struggles and hardships of a Ukrainian girl who pushed against the odds to bring her big and impossible American dream to life would connect with all those people.

Not only did it allow me to improve my English (I barely spoke it when I first arrived to America), but it also gave me the platform to gain my voice.

The more I spoke publicly, sharing my stories, the more opportunities I created for myself. Eventually, I managed to define my signature proposition and the value I create with my business.

There is so much power in owning our stories. They heal us. They inspire others. They give hope. They create exposure.

## Where do you begin to define your voice?

There is a story, and there is a story that connects and influences. What makes the difference is how you infuse your identity with your story. When you care about something deeply, you transfer your personality on the page.

Your voice has the ability to take the raw material and turn it into shape, giving it substance and meaning. The activating force is passion.

Voice is a personality on the page. When you find your voice, your people will find you.

I am going to share some practical strategies on how to develop your own voice. However, I want you to use them with a playful attitude.

Turn the process of discovery into an enjoyable and playful experience. Play is at the heart of creativity. As soon as you give yourself permission to play, ideas will start to flow. The state of flow is the most conducive to creating an interesting and vivid story. And the more stories you create, the more you become aware of your unique voice.

Be patient with yourself if you feel you've got your inner genius ready to burst from the deep place of inspiration, but you find it difficult to put in the right words in a compelling shape or form that will grow its legs.

By engaging in the process of practising sharing your stories, you unleash the glorious.

A beautiful story must be coaxed out of you. And it requires practice and guidance.

There is no glory in practice, but glory is impossible without practice.

Remember, you always accelerate the process when you have a mentor helping you shape your voice.

## From running away off the stage to becoming an international speaker

When I was a child, I had no voice. Literally.

When I was nine years old, I was asked to recite a poem at my mom's church. I remember the meticulous preparation of hours of learning and rehearsing. On a Sunday morning, I was prepared. I knew the poem by heart (I had rehearsed for what seemed like thousands of times), and I had a backup plan: I had a piece of paper with a written poem on it tucked in the sleeve of my sweater.

When I got on stage, my heart dropped to my feet. I could feel my sweaty palms and a chill down my spine. I had a hard time breathing. All forty people in that enormously huge audience were looking at me. I didn't know how to place my feet so I wouldn't look embarrassed. My knees were shaking. I had a million thoughts in my mind, none of which made any sense or could help calm my looming anxiety.

I wanted to run away, but I couldn't. I was frozen and couldn't move.

So I start speaking. A few lines in, I think, it's going well. And then — blank. I don't remember what goes next. "Oh God, help me." I start frantically praying in my head. But there is nothing. Silence. Void. Forty pairs of eyes are fixated on me. Are they judging me? Come on, God, where are you? Out of all places, I am at church. My mind is exploding.

I am holding on to that piece of paper in the sleeve of my sweater, but I am unable to move and dare to break the silence, embarrassing myself even more. I try to open my mouth to apologise or say something to fix the situation, but I can't utter a single sound. I have no voice. Literally.

A few moments drag on like an eternity, and I make the final decision. I run away, full of shame, swallowing the bitter tears of disappointment.

Apparently, God was busy with a more important occasion, so didn't have time to attend to my prayer request.

I had to learn the lesson myself, the meaning of which I unpacked only in my mid-twenties.

Despite that dismal failure with public speaking, somehow, my purpose found its way back into my life.

When I moved to America, in the midst of my self-searching, I discovered my passion for stories. I was devouring the books where authors shared their stories of failures and triumphs, the stories of victories and overcoming obstacles. They spoke to me at a soul level, awakening new facets of my awareness and desire.

Perhaps, I could do the same?

I became a member of the Toastmasters organisation (a public speaking club) and started timidly sharing my stories. I was awkward and rubbish, frankly. I still have those cringe-worthy videos of my first public presentations. However, people in the audience were supportive and encouraging, for whom I am eternally grateful.

In August 2015, I attended the International Leadership Conference. I loved the event and everything about it: the people, the energy and the atmosphere. But most of all, I was mesmerised by the powerful speakers. They were so confident and full of grace when sharing their transformational messages. I could clearly see the transformation happening in front of my own eyes. It was magical.

Personal growth live events are my healthy drug. It's amazing how inspired and insightful people get during those live events. They help you realign with your life purpose and see that all of your challenges have a perfect place on your journey, because if it weren't for those experiences, you wouldn't be where you are now.

Steve Jobs said, "You cannot connect the dots looking forward. You can only connect them by looking backwards. But the dots will always connect for you." In that live training, I knew my dots were connecting right that moment.

I dared to dream bigger. I dared to see myself clearly on that beautiful stage, with a microphone, with a happy and smiley face in front of thousands of people, confident and in my sweet spot. I vividly pictured my dream coming true.

It felt beautiful. But at the same time, I started hearing the negative voices in my head. "How am I going to get on that stage? I don't have any specialised expertise. I don't have much speaking experience. I don't have transformational messages. English isn't my first language, for goodness' sake. Who am I to be selected to speak at the International Conference?"

Six months later, after hard work, determination, and persistence, I was one of only five people (outside the celebrity speakers and the faculty mentors of that organisation) selected to be on that stage. I had the honour and the privilege, not only to share my message with about 2000 people from more than 100 different countries in the world, which was magical, but also to share the stage with John Maxwell, Nick Veicjic, Les Brown and other world-class influencers.

I was determined to discover my voice while sharing my stories. I was willing to grow through the process. Although my growth journey was at the infant stages when I had that triumphant moment on a big stage, it served as a testament to my dedication. By consistently practising my craft and actively showing up, I gradually began to define and refine my unique voice.

Just like you learn to ride a bike by actually riding a bike, you define your voice by sharing your stories publicly. With social media channels, everybody has a platform to share their voice through stories. The only thing that could potentially stop you from getting your message to the world is you. Don't let your past failures stop you from reaching your destiny.

## What is UNIQUE?

What does it mean to be unique? Let's unpack it.

> To be unique, your story must have these elements:
>
> **U**niversal Truth
>
> **N**ovelty
>
> **I**ngenious Insight
>
> **Q**uality Value
>
> **U**nified Transformation
>
> **E**mpowerment

*Universal truth.* What is the truth you are here to share?

Does your story have a universal appeal, something we all can relate to? What does your story tell us about what it means to be human?

People are hungry to connect with those who can shed light on the truth. People are willing and ready to pay a lot of money to help them bring clarity to their challenges and share the light on workable solutions.

Perhaps, the most liberating and freeing moment in life is the "moment of truth" that illuminates our lives, disperses confusion, and clarifies what must be done. This is the moment when a person clearly sees the next step in their transformation. Your job as a storyteller is to facilitate that moment.

How do you do it? Speak profoundly into what is possible, awakening and stirring something within.

*Novelty.* What is the novelty? A story is about originality, not duplication. It has to reflect you, your hero's journey, and your path of overcoming. However, you need to know how to link it to your customers' needs and wants to make it relevant to them. To tackle this challenge, you must become really clear on the problem that keeps them stuck and the outcome they want to achieve.

Find an angle that's different to conventional wisdom to speak into their pain and pleasure. What keeps them trapped and what would bring relief? Shocking statements, provocative questions, and unexpected approaches that get attention, trigger curiosity and compel behaviour will help you bring the novelty element to your story.

If you were your own customer, what would grab your attention?

*Insight.* What captures your imagination producing your own ingenious insights? A story of staggering power and beauty has got to have an ingenious insight.

In order to express an insight, you need to learn to create a balance between facts and truths. A "fact" is what happens. A "truth" is what we think about what happens. And that's where you draw your insight.

> *"If you take any activity, any art, any discipline, any skill — take it and push it as far as it will go, push it beyond where it has never been before, push it to the wildest edges of edges, then you force it into the realm of magic."* - **Tom Robbins**

*Quality value.* What quality value can you provide?

Where have you spent time mastering a subject that you could talk about for hours, sharing your expertise? What is it you could talk about in your sleep?

What kind of expert would you call yourself?

Where is that sweet spot where your capabilities and passions merge?

How aware are you of your gifts and how viable they are in the marketplace?

These are thought-provoking questions that dig deep. They are not on the surface level. But once you find clear answers, you will define your unique voice.

***Unified transformation.*** Let's focus on identifying the common thread that unifies your transformation. While there are many factors that contribute to personal growth and development, there is often one overarching theme that ties them together.

Perhaps it is a relentless pursuit of self-improvement or a steadfast commitment to personal values. Maybe it's a willingness to take risks or a belief in the power of positive thinking. Whatever it may be, identifying this common thread can help you better understand the drivers of your transformation and communicate them to others.

When sharing stories, it's important to keep this common thread in mind. What strategies, beliefs, or practices have been most instrumental in your own transformation? How can you share these insights with others in a way that is both accessible and actionable?

Reflecting on your own journey can also be a powerful tool for self-growth. Imagine writing a love letter to your younger self, filled with words of encouragement and wisdom. What would you say to inspire and motivate yourself during difficult times? How can you use this same language to uplift others who are struggling?

Take some time and write a love letter to yourself. It will bring you clarity on how to connect with others. Chances are, other people struggle with the same issues that you did.

Remember, your own story is a powerful tool for inspiring transformation in others. By sharing your experiences, insights, and strategies, you can help others create the change they desire.

***Empowerment.*** Clarifying the unified transformation will allow you to articulate how your story empowers others. How can you communicate your message in a way that connects with their experiences and makes them feel empowered to create change in their own lives?

One key to empowerment is helping your audience connect with their own power. This may involve sharing specific strategies, tools, or techniques that have been effective for you, or simply sharing your own experiences in a way that encourages others to take action.

Remember, the goal is not to tell others what to do, but to inspire and motivate them to find their own path towards transformation. By sharing your story with honesty and vulnerability, you can create a safe space for others to explore their own journey of growth and self-discovery.

Does your story have these elements: **U**niversal Truth, **N**ovelty, **I**ngenious **I**nsight, **Q**uality Value, **U**nified Transformation, and **E**mpowerment?

Creativity, as well as success, are not linear. "Messy" is an accurate description of the process. The point is to enjoy your mess, which eventually turns into a beautiful message.

The process, however, becomes much easier and more enjoyable when you have expert guidance.

Send me an email at anna@anna-simpson.com, so we can talk to see if there is a fit.

## 9 Strategies to develop your voice

Here are nine simple yet powerful strategies to develop your own unique voice.

1. *Share an original perspective.* To be different and unique, it is not necessary to create something absolutely original or come up with a brand-new idea. You just need to be able to find your unique perspective, which is fresh, textured and activating. Stories are a brilliant tool to do this effectively. Stories are repeated, passed on and transformed. At the end of the day, we all have one story to tell — becoming the "hero" in our life, conquering all villains, but what makes each story different is our unique perception of our circumstances and challenges. The stories of overcoming are the most powerful because they give the rest of us hope. Capture the reflections on your own emotions and responses. Learn to identify and articulate your own truth.

2. *Pay attention to details.* In your quest to develop your own voice, learn to pay attention to small details others don't pay attention to. Turn on your observation, keep your eyes and ears open, and be on alert for the stories that surround you. You might see a different angle on the same old picture. Most of the pictures you see will be fairly ordinary, but one of them will be as close to perfect as you'll ever get. Sometimes, one detail can make all the difference, just one idea can change the entire life. Learn to capture moments, transferring insight and emotion.

3. *Learn the art of description.* Use a creative approach and your own manner of thinking and talking, not just a formal tone. Do not underestimate how much you know. Get curious about describing what you have experienced. Use

all your five senses when describing. In such a way, you invite people into your world, making them fully experience your ideas. Do not be afraid to expose your quirks. Your people will connect with you and will love your quirks. That's what makes us different. When you find it hard to find the right words for your ideas, say them out aloud. Record yourself. Karl Weick wisely observed, "How can I know what I think until I see what I say?" That's how you make sense. You listen to yourself, you articulate your thoughts, and you get to see what you are trying to say. You will be amazed at the insights you will get when you engage in this simple yet fun process. You will be able to hear the clues for a better understanding of your voice, and you will become aware of the ways to make your expression more intense, juicy and insightful.

4. *Persuade yourself first.* If you are not sold on your ideas, you simply cannot sell them to anybody else. People always do one thing for one reason only: because they feel like it. We love movies because they move us from the inside. In order to persuade others, you have to move them emotionally. Do not start writing and creating when you are not moved. When you are moved on the inside, you can transfer that energy to others. With your stories, your job is to make people feel like it is going to change their life. There are two ways you can move your audience. The first one is to offer a big promise that gives your audience an inspirational sense of what they might be able to have. The second one is to highlight their problem, aggravate it and then offer a solution. It is about the balance between building excitement and playing on fear. Do them in equal measure in a way that your potential customer feels safe. When you

can cause your audience to feel excited and a little scared of missing out, you have mastered the art of persuasion.

5. *Fall in love with telling your own stories.* The world wants to buy the inner hero, not the inner copycat. When you share your own authentic stories, nobody can copy you. When you do it long enough, your style becomes refined, and your voice becomes distinguished. Always tell the truth. The interesting thing about truth is that it is not necessarily what actually happened. Sometimes, even actual events or real dialogue fail to ring true in a story. Life is often boring, but the art of storytelling makes it meaningful. Telling your story, share your truth. Always make a point. Never ramble. Be concise and on target. Share only relevant and on the need-to-know basis details in the story. According to John Updike, stories are a kind of rough diamond, "fragments chipped from experiences and rounded by imagination into personal artefacts."

6. *Be a reader.* To develop your own style, you must be an insatiable reader. Become an active reader by drawing and using the wisdom of others, blending it with your own inspiration and voice. By peeking into the great minds of others, you tap the potential with your own inspiration and voice. It sparks your own creative juices, giving you a better vocabulary and a depository of interesting quotes.

7. *Add humour.* Don't be afraid to show your genuine, authentic and, perhaps, silly personality. Humour always disengages ego. When you can laugh at yourself, it is even better. Don't be afraid of being misunderstood or judged. Growing up, I was shy and awkward. I desperately wanted to fit in, but I didn't know how. I couldn't be myself. But then I started looking at my quirks as my asset and turning them into ways to laugh at myself and amuse others. Yes,

on our first romantic holiday with my husband, who was a boyfriend at that time, I walked into a glass door, giving myself a massive bruise on the forehead and a reason for my husband to take the mickey out of me for the rest of the trip. Yes, I can fall off the stairs in the most inappropriate moments, I even tripped on stages while speaking publicly. So what?! I am clumsy. And I find it funny.

8. *Forget confidence; choose action.* Don't make confidence your focus. Don't make overcoming fear your focus. Make action your focus. Don't overcomplicate action. Don't get wrapped up in the mental game. Just do it. Don't try to make it perfect on the first attempt. Even when you don't know what to say, what to share, and how to articulate your ideas, start somewhere. Clarity comes from engagement, not just thinking. Have self-compassion if you don't make 100% progress in a day. Getting better just by 1% every day is a game changer. The way you build confidence is by engaging in purposeful action on a regular basis.

9. *Allow the fruits to ripen.* Enjoy the process. Constantly engage in sharing your authentic self. Remember, you are exactly where you need to be in terms of your awareness and results. One of my beloved clients, Linda, shared a story about growing a citrus grove with orange and lemon trees in her garden. When lemons appeared, they looked like limes, so she plucked them off, thinking she'd bought a lime instead of a lemon tree. But, in fact, those were lemons. She just didn't give them enough time to ripen into juicy, flavourful and ready-to-be-plucked fruits. When you allow the fruits to get ready, they will be scrumptious. If you pick them too soon, they are sour, hard and not juicy. Don't get impatient and frustrated expecting the delicious fruits before they are ready.

## Do you take liberty with the truth?

I have mentioned a few times that it is crucial to share the truth when telling your stories. Let's expand this concept a little deeper.

Is it ok to take liberty with truth for a story effect? I was reflecting on this question after the first written assignment of my Oxford Writing Lives course. We had to describe a memorable event of our life in two ways: the first, as it actually happened, and the second — making some small modifications allowing other students to guess which one was true.

Here is what I wrote.

I am standing in my rose-white wedding dress, holding my pink and white roses, waiting for my Prince Charming. My fiancée had to return to the hotel room (perhaps, he forgot the rings) It is a hot sunny day in West Palm Beach, Florida. We are not going to have a big reception. Just some close friends in a spectacular Breaker's restaurant. Quiet, low-key and intimate, celebrating the union of our love. Everything seems and looks perfect. Beautiful sunny day (considering it was raining all week before). I am about to marry the man of my dreams, my best friend and soulmate. Then why am I feeling out of sorts? It isn't just bridal nerves. It is something else. But I can't exactly pinpoint the root. My friend, Julia, and Richard, the photographer, keep taking pictures of me, complimenting my appearance and making me feel special.

Where is he? I am thinking. We are going to be late for our wedding reception. Ten minutes turn into twenty, and my anxiety grows exponentially. Everything is perfect, but is it …? I decide to run up the room and get him myself. I open our hotel room. It is the same but different at the same time. His stuff is gone, including the suitcase. There is a note on a coffee table — so sorry...

Wait, what?

I am not sure what I am feeling.

And I start uncontrollably laughing.

I go to the walk-in closet, open it, and a warm wave of relief engulfs me. He is standing there with a mischievous grin. "What took you so long?" he says, and we both can't stop laughing. "You knew you were dating a bugger with a wicked sense of humour who will never stop playing you up."

We embrace each other in the biggest hug, making our connection even tighter.

And yes, the day is absolutely perfect. The adrenaline shot added a little bit of spice.

Do you think this is the actual story of my life? As a matter of fact, yes. It actually happened.

However, I took some acceptable liberty with the truth for a dramatic effect of the story. In reality, Christian (my husband's name) had been playing me up for the entire week before our wedding day with his cheeky attitude, saying he still had time to escape the ball and chain, jokingly reminding himself to book the plane tickets back to London. He was making sure I could hear his intentions. It was a laughing subject for the entire week.

So, the "surprise" on the wedding day wasn't as unexpected. On the big day, I went to get my hair and make-up done at the salon. Upon returning, I found our hotel room empty and a note on a coffee table: "so sorry".

That's when I opened the closet, and there the bugger was. I wasn't hysterically laughing; I wasn't petrified either. I was expecting it.

After I found my clown in the closet, we had a few giggles, and then we got dressed and walked down the stairs to the hotel lobby together, holding hands and enjoying every moment of the official inception of our family.

For the sake of the story, I decided to add some colours and dramatic effects to make it more interesting.

Life is often boring and usually falls flat if you stick just to the facts. Little modifications, embellishment of emotions and extra colour will breathe life into your story. That doesn't mean you alter the truth completely. Attending Harvard University on a school trip doesn't make you an honorary Harvard graduate. Spending a night in prison isn't the same as hard prison time (not quite sure why this example came to mind, but you get my point)!

## Turn theory into practice

To turn theory into practice when discovering your voice, you must actively engage in the actual writing.

Before I share your first writing assignment, you must put yourself in the right frame of mind.

Detach yourself from any negative thinking or negative voices. Release self-judgement and comparisons with others. There are always going to be people who are further down the path and who you might think are much better communicators or storytellers. You might think their stories are better articulated and more insightful.

The truth is, comparing yourself to others is exactly the same as comparing apples to mangos. They are different. Just like our journey is different to others. And we have to own where we are.

The only fair comparison is you to you, your past self to your present self. Honour yourself for how far you have come.

Clearly set an intention, "I have something to say." This intention must truly resonate with you. Literally say to yourself, "I have a voice to share."

And then, write a short essay, "Who am I?"

Don't try to make it perfect. You are not writing the copy for your "about me" website or the first chapter of your memoir. Do not fret about using beautiful language with colourful metaphors and other clever literary devices. The purpose of this is to activate your ability to express yourself. Just pour out your heart and let your mind flow into expressing who you believe you are.

Here are some assisting points you might want to write about if you experience "blank page" syndrome.

Think of the three qualities you believe best describe you and your character. Why have you chosen those particular features? Pick some stories, events or examples with texture, details and insights where you demonstrate those qualities. Reflect on how those qualities served or didn't serve you. Write your thoughts down.

If you want to take this deeper, talk about your shadows and their purpose in your life. Shadows usually represent darker or more challenging parts of our lives, personalities or experiences. These shadows can refer to unresolved emotions, hidden fears, past traumas, or negative patterns of behaviour. They symbolise the parts of ourselves that we may try to avoid, ignore, or suppress. Find an angle at how your shadows enable your light. How do you feel about them? Do they liberate or constrain you? Where do you feel resistance? Are you in a harmonious state of alignment? Capture those thoughts in writing.

Formulate a spectacle of yourself, sharing the remarks about yourself and expressing your character. Describe some accurate, specific events as well as your subjective impressions on the meaning of those events. Become curious about yourself. Define what's really important. Distinguish between noise and insight. And soon enough, your narrative will begin to flow.

When you read stories that captivate your imagination and connect with your soul, you either consciously or unconsciously join the characters inside the tale, believing in the way they think and feel about their past, present and future. You pay attention to the balance between action and retrospection and how introspection mixed with external engagement creates transformation.

Now it is your turn to think of your own character as someone who will captivate the imagination of others and connect with their soul.

Allow yourself to lean into the process of self-discovery. It might take you to soulful confessions, the journey of healing and forgiveness and the realisation of your own transformation. It might take you to some completely unexpected but beautiful 'aha moments'.

Don't be afraid to go deep. Be intimate, vulnerable and genuine. You don't have to publicly share your essay if it makes you feel uncomfortable.

The next part of this assignment is to think of the three qualities other people would describe you. Reflect on whether your own perception of yourself corresponds with how others perceive you. It will expand your awareness about how you show up and how you reveal your authentic self to the world.

Then write about what you passionately believe in. Express strong emotions of joy, anger, justice, passion, and pride. What makes you happy? Write about joy without mentioning the word. What about ecstasy? What lifts your spirits to enormous heights?

What makes you scared? Describe your feelings. Emotion is the heart of voice.

Approach this exercise with a playful attitude. Have fun with it. Give yourself the luxury of engaging in "you time".

This exercise is effective in drawing your authentic truth, understanding who you are and articulating your own insights. You will learn how to hear and connect with yourself, how to give voice to your thoughts and feelings and how to identify your own writing style.

I always gravitate towards an inspirational style in my writing, teaching and speaking. Whether I share a story, an idea or an insight, my intention is to inspire people to think bigger of themselves by being, doing and having more. My vehicle of transformation is stories in the context of personal growth and business building.

What is your style?

Take some time to reflect on your essay. What does it reveal to you about yourself and your voice?

## Refine your voice by looking for a deeper meaning

When one of my mentors, Simon Bowen, said, "Sexy sells but profound will outsell sexy every time of the week", and it instantly resonated with me. I have always been attracted to uncovering the deep meaning of things instead of dwelling on shallow and stereotypical perceptions, even when it was challenging.

It started in my university years when I was in Ukraine.

As soon as the tutor walked into the auditorium with bright orange hair as if it was on fire, deep blue eyes that could see what was invisible to others, and plain, almost ascetic clothes, I could feel we were up for an exhilarating journey.

She looked like a witch (in the most positive sense of a word), giving the impression that she had access to eternal wisdom or some kind of holy grail. Her calm demeanour, sophisticated language, original approach to perceiving things and insatiable curiosity were the tell-tale signs that it was going to be a fantastic course. Her name was Miss Lidia.

I have always loved books, and I was intrigued by developing my critical thinking with that course.

However, I nearly failed that class in the first semester. Miss Lidia had the reputation of being from another planet, and very few could really get on the wavelength of her thinking. Later in life, I understood the problem was that Miss Lidia did not tolerate students who refused to think for themselves and who would read some critical reviews rather than develop their own understanding of the read books.

You either loved or hated her. There was no in-between. Most students hated her because thinking is one of the hardest things to do.

She would always encourage her students to look for meaning from an unconventional perspective, to connect the dots in a different way, to expand and grow their imagination, and to connect with their thoughts and ideas on a different level.

At first, I had a little understanding of what "looking for a deeper meaning" meant, and how it would assist me in passing the class in practical terms. It wasn't enough to just read a novel and learn about the characters, their problems and the obvious lessons. We were meant to somehow arrive at a profound insight level that wasn't explicitly depicted but that was supposed to be drawn from within.

Now, looking back, I smile, thinking those were my first attempts at self-coaching, connecting and drawing from internal wisdom.

Miss Lidia was not just a teacher of literature; she was a teacher of true Socratic thinking.

I am so grateful to her for lighting up those sparks of curiosity within me to turn them into a mighty flame of a lifetime quest for truth and profound insights.

This is why I absolutely love the statement, "Sexy sells, but profound will outsell sexy any time of the week."

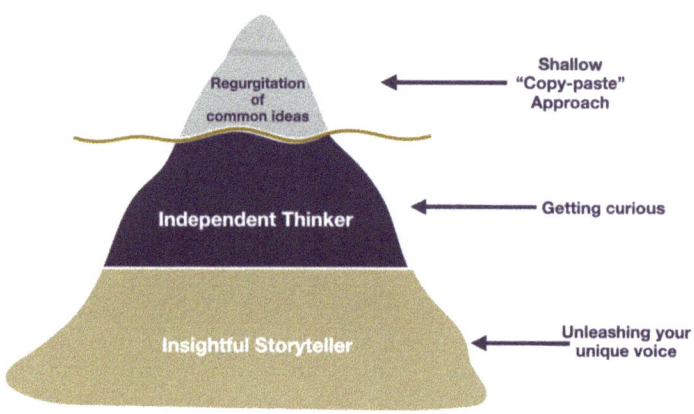

If we look at the visual model, on the shallow level, we see the regurgitation of common ideas. Most people are incapable of original and interesting thinking; they'd rather resort to the copy-paste approach. It seems easier, but it's not effective. Catchy phrases, crisp punch lines and loud but empty promises might get attention, but because of the lack of substance, they don't bring any value. They don't really capture the imagination and engage behaviour.

If we go a little deeper, we get to the level of an independent thinker, where there are some attempts of a curious approach of trying to explain things in a different way, looking for what is not spoken. It might be an interesting or clever expression, but if you don't mix your character and personality, it might fail to ring true in the eyes of an audience.

How do you create a meaningful connection? By sharing your truth through your authentic voice.

We have talked about the tools and tactics to develop your unique voice. Now it is time to put them to practice. Through relentless practice and not being afraid of being judged and misunderstood, you courageously step on a quest to seek and express your message. And if you stay true to the process, you arrive at that profound level of what I call becoming an insightful storyteller.

When you accept this quest, you begin to question everything and perceive everything through your own lenses of understanding and judgement. You do not blindly follow any guru. You get inspired by them and their wisdom, but you make sure you arrive at your own wisdom and your own perspective.

The challenge is to dig deeper to articulate your knowledge, experience and intuitive understanding in a unique way. You do it by challenging the status quo, experimenting with your writing and creativity, and getting invaluable feedback from a mentor.

You develop your expertise through application. Storytelling ability is no different to any other skill. If you have come to the influencer market to create a lasting impact, not just a short-term gain, you have to dedicate your time and effort to refining your voice.

## An elephant and a dog story. Or don't kill your growth with impatience

We live in a society with immediate gratification expectations. The world where everything is just a click away makes people impatient. Everyone wants results, but very few are prepared to go through the process that brings them.

If you take a right intentional action (outlined in this book), I can promise you, you will elevate your influence, attract the right clients and increase your income.

However, I am very clear that this is not the magic bullet. You have to put in your efforts and do the work, even if you decide to be mentored by me.

Here is an inspirational story by an unknown author I came across on the internet.

An elephant and a dog became pregnant at the same time. Three months down the line, the dog gave birth to six puppies. Six months later, the dog was pregnant again, and nine months on, it gave birth to another dozen puppies. The pattern continued.

On the eighteenth month, the dog approached the elephant, questioning, "Are you sure that you are pregnant? We became pregnant on the same date, I have given birth three times to a dozen puppies, and they are now grown to become big dogs, yet you are still pregnant. What's going on?"

The elephant replied, "There is something I want you to understand. What I am carrying is not a puppy but an elephant.

I only give birth to one in two years. When my baby hits the ground, the earth feels it.

When my baby crosses the road, human beings stop and watch in admiration; what I carry draws attention. So what I'm carrying is mighty and great."

The moral of the story is — do not get despondent. Don't lose faith when you see others achieving their success. Don't be envious of others' results.

If you haven't received your success, don't despair.

Say to yourself, "My time is coming, and when it hits the surface of the earth, people shall yield in admiration."

Everything worthwhile takes effort, flexibility, commitment and the right guidance.

## Summary points

- Discovering your voice begins with owning your story.
- Infuse your personality with your story.
- Approach the process with a playful attitude. Play unleashes creativity.
- Be UNIQUE. To be unique, your story must have **u**niversal truth, contain the element of **n**ovelty, inspire **i**ngenious **i**nsight, provide **q**uality value, speak into **u**nified transformation and **e**mpower your audience.
- Use these strategies to develop your voice: share an original perspective, pay attention to details, learn the art of description, persuade yourself first, fall in love with telling your own stories, be a reader, add humour, forget confidence; choose action, allow the fruits to ripen.
- It is okay to take liberty with truth for a story effect as long as you don't change the facts completely.
- Develop your own style of expression by actively engaging in writing actual personal stories that reflect you and your character with warts and all.
- Refine your voice by looking for a deeper meaning behind events and experiences.
- Everything worthwhile takes effort, flexibility, commitment and the right guidance. Do not get despondent and trust the process.

# 5
# How Do You Articulate it so People Pay Attention?

*"Make it simple. Make it memorable. Make it inviting to look at. Make it fun to read."* **Leo Burnett**

The most challenging part about storytelling is finding the right words that connect with people's hearts and open their wallets.

How do you articulate your stories in a clear and concise way, compelling people to take action?

Let's talk about the copywriting fundamentals that will massively improve your ability to communicate.

First of all, what is copywriting? Copywriting is the ability to create persuasive content for marketing and advertising purposes. In other words, copywriting is the ability to find the right words that sell.

The entire purpose of sharing your transformational hero stories is not to engage in a creative project but to persuade people to work with you because what you have to offer can change their life. Your job is just to make them believe your offer is exactly what they've been looking for.

Let me be very clear, I am not talking about manipulation. You manipulate someone when you convince them to do something they don't want to do. There are many people using misleading, manipulative and even malicious techniques.

What I am going to share with you in this chapter will help you to ethically influence people's behaviour. If you have integrity and you are focused on making a difference, you will find the following principles and tools invaluable. Influencing people to make decisions that are in their best interests is the most lucrative skill you can ever develop.

You have to master the fundamentals of what you are saying, how you are saying it, who is listening and why they should care.

## Never push. Create flow

Once, I came across an online marketer doing a presentation with the intention to sell his high-ticket program. What really caught my attention is the way he was speaking to his audience. He was aggressive, arrogant and extremely pushy. He was practically barking at people. I immediately got turned off. I don't know anything about the value he offers with his products or services. But I was not even interested in finding out what he had to offer. The way he treated people showed massive disrespect. I got the impression it was all about the money for him and making the numbers.

There is nothing wrong with your desire to create financial abundance. But if it is all about you and your outcomes, people feel your attitude and intentions, and it becomes easier for them to disengage.

It actually made me think about the paradox of power. The harder we push, the more likely we are to be met with resistance.

People don't like to be pushed. It creates pressure and resistance. When you push, you activate a psychological force that will pull people away from you. People want to be understood and valued.

Your job is to position your value in an irresistible way so that your people will make the decision you want them to make — to get into your world, buy your product, or sign up for your offer.

In our Conscious Coaching Academy, we call this approach the Aikido way. The Aikido Way is about influence without power, control without force, and transformation without projection.

The thing is, you create resistance if you push your agenda on your audience. You create flow when you shift the focus from yourself to your customer and their journey.

You learn the art and science of an irresistible positioning when you learn to speak the language your audience understands.

In Robert Collier's words, "You need to enter the conversation already taking place in the customer's mind." Collier believed that to find customers, persuade them to follow you, and hopefully change their lives with the products and services you sell, you need to know and understand them better than they understand themselves.

## How well do you know your audience?

How well can you articulate their pain? How skilfully can you paint the picture of the transformation they desire?

What do they really want?

What are they afraid of?

Answering these questions with clarity will give you clues about your audience's problems and desires. Knowing their problems and desires will help you build a connection with them through your stories.

Get really clear on the language they use to describe their problems and desires.

Many coaches say, "I help my clients tap their unlimited potential". I am not quite sure what it means. Or, another one — Step into your power… Again, it is ambiguous. I highly doubt that people wake up in the morning with the thoughts, "Right. Today I am going to work on expanding my potential." Or "I wonder how to step into my power."

The problem with the vague statements, well, they are vague. They could mean a plethora of different things.

And people don't resonate with vague statements. They look for concrete details that paint a picture.

Here is an example: "I was in a dark place."

Can you imagine what it looks like?

Well, there could be a number of different things. It could mean I was consumed by depression after losing my grandmother. It could be that I was sleeping till noon, not showering for a week and wearing my dirty pyjamas all the time. Or it could mean I was in a dimly lit bar, drinking a mojito.

How to fix ambiguous language? Answer the question, "What does it look like?"

Replace ambiguous with something more palatable. Give concrete specifics that describe their pain and discomfort and give the promise of transformation. People buy for two reasons. One is to solve their problems. Two is to achieve their desired outcomes.

In order to connect with your audience, you first need to show you understand their struggles. Your copy must make them say, "You truly get me. That's exactly where I am at and how I feel."

Show them you understand their character, their personality, what makes them tick, and what they think about when stuck in traffic. Describe the conflict between their desires and their current state.

## Build an emotional connection

Nothing evokes more emotions than the description of the conflict.

Hone in on what it is like "to be in the trenches", and share some poignant details of the conflict they inevitably face. When you share your story of overcoming — from being in the trenches to getting the reward — you create an emotional journey. You make them understand that you are just like them. What charges up emotion is a powerful description of the conflict with relevant details that bring the story to life and build trust with your audience.

When you connect with them at the problem level, then introduce a new opportunity (your service) that will change everything for them. No matter how many failed attempts they have had before. Persuade them, this time, it is going to be different. Because you have proof that your methodology works (your own story and the stories of your clients).

You introduce a new opportunity when you paint a clear picture of transformation. That picture of transformation answers the question, "When they cross the bridge from pain to pleasure, what will reality look like?"

Your promise of transformation needs to produce a liberating effect. So they can say, "Aww, that's exactly what I want. I couldn't have articulated it better. How do I sign up?"

An effective marketing copy contains the following elements: problem, desire and story. All these aspects have to be relevant to your audience and activated by emotion. Make them feel the excitement of the prospect of working with you.

*"You never really understand a person until you consider things from his point of view. Until you climb inside his skin and walk around it."* - **Harper Lee**

Study their pains, recognise their fears, muse on their dreams. It's not easy to slip into someone else's swimsuit, it doesn't always fit right, and sometimes their style just makes no sense to us. But it's a key part (if not the key) of creating content that drives action. And we can't do it without key emotion. Humans are emotional beings, and they always make decisions based on emotions. Only then, they justify it with logic.

Most people try to connect on an intellectual level with their audience by talking about the details of their programs. They attempt to sound interesting, smart and punchy.

Although it is crucial for your copy to be well-written with a clear positioning of your value, if you want to convert your audience into your clients, you must create an emotional connection.

By getting mentally and emotionally involved with the story, people are much more likely to take action on what they read or listen to.

A story is the most direct route to another person's unconscious mind. Stories stir up fears and desires much more reliably than statements of fact, claims of benefit or empty hollow phrases — all of which you see far too often in copy that doesn't work very well.

## A practical exercise

Unlock your ability to communicate how you can help your audience. Bring them from darkness to light. Fight for them; push them; help them become better versions of themselves in relation to the product or service you are presenting to them to purchase. Use your story so it can become their story of triumph.

The vehicle to build connection, paint a picture of transformation and persuade them to take action is a story. When you master the power of communicating your story, you crack the code of influence, and you can take people where you want them to go.

Michael Hauge (an American Hollywood story consultant) said, "Every good story is about a captivating character who is pursuing some compelling desire and who faces seemingly insurmountable obstacles to achieving it. That's it. If you've got those three things, then you've got a good story."

It is exactly the same in a good copy. You must speak to a compelling character (clearly defined audience), who is on a mission to achieve a desire but faces exasperating internal and external challenges. Describe it. What does it look like? What does it feel like?

People want to be led; they want to be taken somewhere. Clearly articulate what that path looks like by answering the questions, "Why this? Why now? Why you?"

Your ideal client is looking at you. What does she want? Why is it important to her? What is she afraid of? Why hasn't she achieved her desires yet? What is her desire? What conflict is she facing? Why will your product change everything for her?

Write a compelling copy that will open her heart and mind by answering these questions. Keep in mind the service you provide, while writing this copy.

## How to enhance your copy. Focus on benefits, not features

A clear understanding of what your product or service offers to a specific audience is crucial to creating a compelling copy than sells.

If you wish to awaken a response from your audience, you have to communicate from a "what's in it for them" perspective. You must be able to clearly answer the question, "Why should they care?" when you invite them to your world. How do you do it? By focusing on benefits.

People are more naturally wired to share features. But the magic is in the benefits.

What is the difference?

A feature is a description of what a product or service does. A benefit is a description of why those features matter and how they can help a customer. A feature is a detail of the product. A benefit is what the consumer gets from this detail.

Take a simple example of headphones. Wireless is a description of a feature. No more tangled cords is a description of a benefit.

Another example is a meal plan. Feature: arrive ready to heat. Benefit: save time cooking.

If you want to be effective with your communication, you must focus on positioning benefits.

A benefit is what makes something useful to someone. It answers the question, "What's in it for me?"

Again, a feature is "this razor has seven blades". A benefit is "get the smoothest shave of any razor you have ever used."

This car has 4-cylinder twin-turbo engines that have 6-cylinder power is definitely a feature. It is impressive, but how is it useful for a consumer? Unless you "engineer" speak, such description won't make any sense to you. What it actually means is the ability to enjoy a high-performance car that's great for mileage, fuel efficiency and with a high input in torque.

You massively enhance your product or service when you think in terms of benefits rather than features.

It doesn't mean you skip the features. The details are important only when there is a clear and compelling emphasis on their benefits for the customer.

People often use, what I call, empty words: new, special, better, powerful, life-changing, etc. It is all great, but what exactly does it mean?

Benefits provide the context of how the product or service will improve their life.

When you share a story to support the benefits of your product or service, you actually create magic. Stories help you illustrate benefits with real-life scenarios. Remember a great storytelling adage, "show versus tell"? For a great story, you need both. In the context of features and benefits, "telling" is a feature and "showing" is a benefit.

Benefits remind customers of the problems they already have, and how your product or service can help them solve those problems. Benefits address their needs, creating the resonance necessary for them to take action.

When you learn the art and science of communicating the benefits in a clear and concise way, you tackle the alchemy of copywriting. In a nutshell, great copywriting is the ability to clearly communicate needs, desires and solutions to problems of a specific audience.

A perfect customer is someone who needs your product. You can reach them by showing the benefit of the product.

How to identify the benefit?

You learn to communicate benefits by answering the question, "why is it important? What is it going to give to my customers?"

Clarify the purpose of the product. What is it really designed to do? Dig deep. Sometimes people don't even know how to articulate what they want until you place it in front of them.

Define the path you take them on.

> **Let your message be the lighthouse that guides them through the storm. You must define the storm. You must define the light. You must define the path. Assembling these pieces together creates a compelling marketing copy.**

How do you dig deeper to clarify benefits?

When you have a crystal-clear idea of your audience, you understand what is important to them and what will attract their attention.

For example, a new lip gloss with all the natural anti-ageing ingredients *helps you create a gorgeous natural look while taking care of your skin and slowing down the ageing process. You deserve better quality cosmetics. You deserve to look beautiful and young. Get this lip gloss today to boost your self-confidence, making you feel ready to take on the world.*

In this simple example, we tell a self-conscious woman (the target audience) a story about the things she deeply cares about:

her looks, youth and health. But the deepest benefit is making her feel confident by emphasising her natural beauty.

To clearly identify the benefits for your target market, you have to understand their hopes, dreams, fears and needs. You literally have to enter the conversation in their head to see the world from their perspective in order to be able to tell a story that will deeply resonate with them. Then identify how your benefits address these deep issues.

Benefits allow you to reach your audience on an emotional level. Digging into benefits takes your insight into a deeper understanding of your audience's life. You must clearly and compellingly communicate how your product will make a difference in their lives.

## Add fire to your copy

If your business challenges the status quo; if you don't offer the same commoditised solution to the old problem; if you are different from others; you must show it. And you show it by showing up differently.

A powerful way to propel your influence on the market is by showing your passion. When you deeply care about your cause, people must feel your fire. Fire is the spark that ignited human evolution.

When our ancestors got control of fire, they could cook food, create warmth and ward off predators at night.

The benefit of fire now is sparking imagination through storytelling.

If you are passionate about your cause, this feeling is contagious. You make your audience feel passionate as well. And, as a result, they want to be part of what it is you are doing because what you do matters.

It speaks to their soul, opens their heart, and resonates with their mind, allowing them to see the value of what you do.

Inspiring storytellers are inspired themselves. They are convinced by their message, clear on their value and driven by inner motivation. They enthusiastically share their passion with the audience.

People are more likely to take risks in a heightened positive state of emotions and take fewer risks when feeling sad. When you ask people to buy something from you, you pose a risk to your audience. Parting with money always creates a certain level of risk for people.

Your copy must make them feel excited, emphasising high benefits and low risks.

Before becoming a problem solver, you have to become a people mover. In other words, people will not open their wallets to you to help them solve their problems unless they are moved. Passion allows you to move people, awaken them from their unconscious living and present a new opportunity to change their life.

Here are some ways to encourage positive emotions in your audience through stories.

Increase their understanding: people love learning new things, especially about themselves.

Support their passionate views. You might be the first person to encourage them to follow their dreams.

Paint a more vivid and evocative picture of possibility. People's perception of what is possible for them is often limited by negative conditioning or by their past failures. In many cases, it is both. Rally for their hidden aspirations.

When you use fear and negative expressions, you must highlight the positive aspect of understanding the problem. For example, "You have this problem. But now that you know it, you can do something about it."

Stay away from empty promises without putting them into context. "You deserve it", "just go for it", "put your mind to it" are shallow slogans.

Truth doesn't come out in bumper stickers (I would actually love this as a bumper sticker, ironically). Your goal is not to encourage entitlement, it is to inspire a rebellion against self-doubt and cancerous delusions of "I just can't do it", along with providing a realistic and easy-to-understand path to success. The truth is — with enough patience and leverage (which is your product or service), almost anyone can accomplish almost anything. It goes without saying that what you promote should do what it promises. There is no need to promise the world; just passionately share how your product will improve their world in the context of what you do.

## Improve your communication

Words matter. The words you choose to tell your story determine the level of its impact.

A great source of inspiration for me to sharpen my language is literature. I am always on the lookout for interesting, evocative and insightful thoughts, words, and expressions, constantly highlighting imaginative turns of phrase. My primary driver is to have a more powerful command of the English language as a non-native speaker.

I encourage you to get curious about words and evocative metaphors and write down interesting ideas and insights.

Get excited about cultivating curiosity for creating the best line to convey the right thought, idea or emotion. Experiment with choosing words that stimulate the senses. Understand words and how they work together. There are certain words that will create the perfect rhythm. It works in poetry, creative writing, storytelling and persuasive copy. It must be smooth. It must be a pleasure to read, to listen to, and to get inspired by.

A method I use is to read out aloud what I write. Sometimes I record myself. Hearing myself helps me determine if it flows.

Be willing to self-edit, looking at your copy with a critical eye. Develop the ability to be concise and succinct. It is better to say less but to the point than more but not totally relevant.

Another effective way to sharpen your language is to look up synonyms to make your ideas more evocative. Look at the following words: sour versus negative. Seize is more expressive than take. Hurl beats throw. Scrumptious is more interesting than tasty.

Be careful with descriptions, though. Although descriptions add colour to your copy, do not overdo it. Many amateur writers sound like they are from the 19-century, deliberately embellishing their sophisticated language, using flowery, elevated, eloquent, but empty words that don't carry any relevant meaning. Isn't it interesting how you can say a lot without conveying anything of meaning?

There are also stock descriptors that pollute the copy. For example, golden sand and endless blue ocean. A copy that states the obvious is boring. Capture your audience with an original description.

Often, the descriptors of attitude do more harm than good. For example, lovely, horrible, unfair, fantastic, amazing, terrible, etc.

When you can replace descriptors with active verbs, it brings your copy to life and creates a stronger effect. 'The light breeze made her hair tangled' could become 'The light breeze tangled her hair'. Verbs are more powerful; they imply action.

I can't talk about sharpening your language, without mentioning cliches. We all use cliches when we talk. "Ants in his pants." "Plenty of fish in the sea." "What goes around comes around." "If only walls could talk."

Cliches get the point across, but they don't spark the imagination. They are like a yellowy-grey worn-out T-shirt. When it was brand new and gleaming white, it looked beautiful, but it has been used and washed so many times that it is dull now. Use your creativity and imagination to find more vivid and original expressions.

## Curiosity triggers

If you want your stories to be effective, you must know how to trigger people's curiosity. The value of curiosity in a marketing copy is indispensable.

What is curiosity? It is having a strong desire to learn or know something. Or in other words, curiosity is like an itch that needs to be scratched.

Curiosity is a key ingredient in influencing human behaviour.

A lot of marketers resort to ridiculous ideas to hook curiosity. Catchy phrases, unrealistic promises, sexy claims… It is all shallow. Our aim is to inspire, entertain, delight and wow our audience at the initial point of contact so they become hungry to learn more.

Here are the practical tips to inspire curiosity in others.

1. Be curious yourself. Change always begins with yourself. How do you activate curiosity? Look for different angles of perception. Your own curiosity quest will give you lots of ideas to captivate the imagination of others. Chances

are, what gets you excited will make others excited as well. You just need to learn to communicate it in the right way.

4. Ask questions and question answers. When Steve Jobs said, "Creativity is just connecting new things", he actually meant "new" things are never actually new. They are just new combinations of the things that already exist. Don't be satisfied with the obvious answers. Look for those unusual, interesting combinations. People's curiosity is sparked by the question, not the answer. People's engagement is kept by open-ended questions and open loops.

5. Practice active listening. When you become intentional at listening to your audience, they will give you clues of what they want and what keeps them stuck. Listen to their language and the choice of their words. Your job is just to find the right way to curiously position it on the market.

6. Look for the hook. What is that one idea, insight, revelation, opportunity, one angle that will make people go, "hmm? I want to learn more about what you talk about." If you knew nothing about your topic, what would capture your imagination? What question, statement, or promise would spark your interest to want to learn more?

Here are four types of curiosity triggers that you can use in your marketing copy.

1. A hidden opportunity in a big area. If your area of expertise covers a big well-known topic, your job is to find a small detail that makes all the difference. It is the place where you create a new opportunity for your audience.

For example, my area of expertise is stories. But it is not a new opportunity. Everybody knows about the significance and impact of stories.

Stories make the world go around, but my intention is to help my audience become a Visionary Guide to their audience through the power of story. It makes people curious about how they can become a Visionary Guide to powerfully influence their audience. Zoom in on one aspect of your proposition and blow it up to create an exciting opportunity for your audience.

2. A big misconception. In a well-known area, there is always room for misunderstanding, mistakes, myths and misconceptions. With the help of this curiosity trigger, you can shed light on a well-known misconception.

Everyone can share a story. But most people don't know how to do it right. They don't know how to influence or sell through a story. They are making common mistakes — making it too long, not including relevant details, and not knowing how to make it authentic, genuine and impactful. The hook here can focus on mistakes. Are you guilty of making one of the common mistakes? Does your story put people to sleep?

With my hero's journey methodology, I show people how to make their audience excited and awaken their desire to work with them. How can you position your story to activate their hero potential and inspire them to work with you? At the end of the day, you share your hero's journey to help them become heroes on their journey to success.

3. Awareness activation. This is the place where you let your people know about how what you do can help them with their desires. In other words, you expand their awareness.

Most people are not aware they have hidden gems in their stories that can massively increase their business results. Did you know you can increase your prices and attract a much better-quality customer if you learn how to share an impactful brand story? Even if you don't believe your origin story is attention-worthy. I can show you how to find the perfect angle in your origin story that will best position your marketing value making people hungry to work with you.

4. Going back to basics. Sometimes, all you have to do is to remind people of the universal truth. Principles of communication, connection and influence are timeless. In today's world of exponential technological advancement, most people are getting lost in sexy marketing platforms, software solutions, shiny object tactics and tools, completely forgetting the basics of what really connects with people's hearts.

This is where the story comes into play. With the help of a well-crafted story, you can get people's attention, make them curious, awaken their desire, show them what's possible and persuade them to work with you.

These simple curiosity triggers are effective tools in hooking people's attention and opening their minds to new ideas or opportunities.

## Summary points

- ❖ Never push your audience. Create flow instead. Shift your focus from yourself to your audience.
- ❖ Get crystal clear on the language your audience uses to describe their problems and desires.
- ❖ Substitute vague and ambiguous statements with specific concrete details that paint a picture to give your message substance.
- ❖ Use vivid details to describe the conflict to build an emotional connection.
- ❖ Clearly answer the question: "When they cross the bridge from pain to pleasure, what will reality look like?"
- ❖ An effective marketing copy contains the following elements: problem, desire and story.
- ❖ Aim to create a liberating effect in your audience, so they can say, "That's exactly what I want. How do we work together?"
- ❖ You must speak to a compelling character (from your clearly defined audience), who is on a mission to achieve a desire but faces exasperating internal and external challenges.
- ❖ To enhance your story, focus on benefits, not features.
- ❖ Add fire to your story. When you deeply care about your cause, people must feel your fire.
- ❖ Improve your expression by being intentional with the words you use.
- ❖ Your story must trigger people's curiosity.

# Choose the Right Future Path

What future are you going to create for yourself? The only thing between your current and future circumstances is the passing of time. Time always wins, and it compounds everything on its path.

Most people think there is a straight line between where you are now and where you will be in the future.

However, the gap between your present and future is never a straight line. It's a curve. And it is either moving up or going down. You are either growing or sliding down.

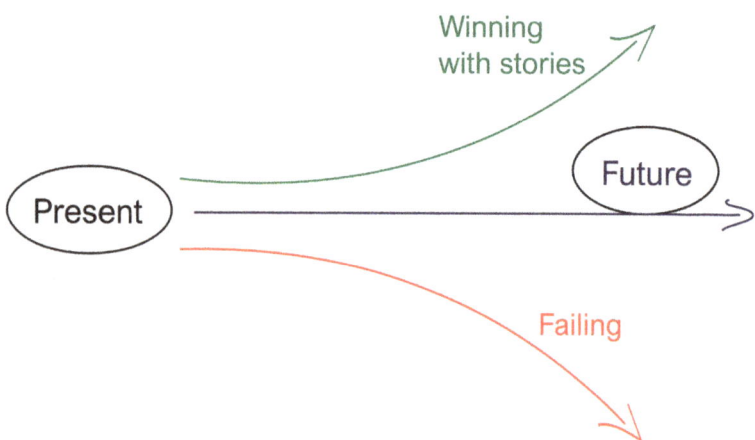

You can either be on the flourishing line going up in the future. Or you can be on the failing line heading down. The flourishing line in the context of what I do is winning with stories. My mission is to ensure you are heading into your future with total confidence in your success. This is the scenario of a bright future where you are using storytelling superpower.

Which future path is more appealing to you?

To enjoy the level of success you know you deserve, you need to make a decision.

The difference between the failing curve going down and the flourishing curve going upward is the difference between drift and decision. By drift I mean passive and unintentional movement without a clear direction or a specific purpose. When people drift in life, they go with the flow, allowing external circumstances to determine their path. The opposite of drift is a decision to become an active creator of your life, not a passive spectator.

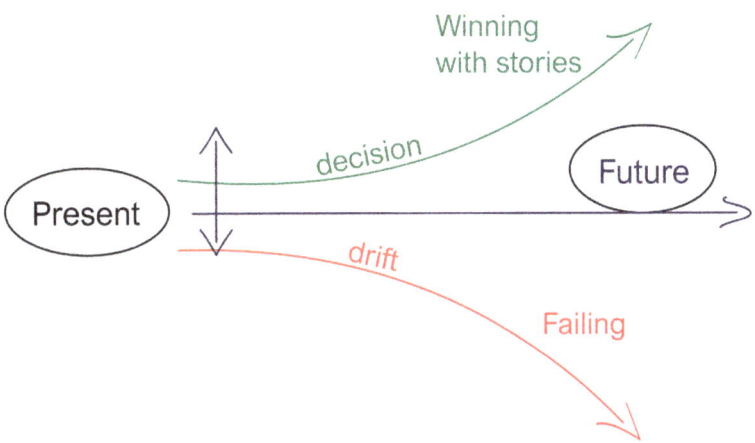

The gap between you and your bright future is in the decisions and the commitment you make to follow through on those decisions.

Are you going to make a decision to jump the lines?

Are you going to make a decision to stay on the line?

The truth is people don't fall off the green line; they behave off the green line. What I mean by that is people deviate from or do not align with the expected or desired behaviour that will take them to their bright future. It is due to their actions and behaviours, rather than a result of randomly "falling off" or losing their way. But if you have a proven system and support to stay on the green line, your future success is a natural consequence.

We have a system with a proven framework and system to help you discover and articulate your message, so you can amplify your influence and results, using stories as your weapon in marketing and content creation.

If you have made it this far in the book, it means its ideas and content have resonated with you. Let's keep the momentum going and explore if there is a fit for us to work together. Respond to any of the emails you receive from me, so we can have a conversation about how you can take all the strategies outlined in the book and your unique situation to the next level.

I believe it is your duty to share your message of light with the world, whatever that is.

As we let our own light shine, we unconsciously give other people permission to do the same. As we become liberated from our own fear, our presence automatically liberates others.

There is enough room for everyone to be influential. There is enough room for everyone to be successful. There is enough room for everyone to be rich. It is only our thinking and a lack of the right tools that block that possibility from happening.

Everyone has a history (High Story). What you do with it is up to you. Some repeat it. Some learn from it. The really special ones use it to help others.

The choice is yours!

# Resources & Support

Check my website: Anna-simpson.com/home to discover additional resources that will help you in your business and life.

Are you interested in creating a transformational impact on people who resonate with your unique voice and message and where you get paid being YOU?

BUT

- You are not able to channel your 'inner hero' power creating your vision-aligned coaching business.
- You are not sure how to articulate the tangible and intangible value that makes your favourite clients say, "How do I work with you?"

- You you feel like you are constantly hustling and failing forward, not getting the results you deserve!

If so, get Anna's help to craft your unique message that reflects your genius and meets a massive need.

For 1:1 Coaching with Anna, please mail Anna directly at anna@anna-simpson.com.

**Discover more about Anna's programs**

*The Blueprint to Radical Confidence*
Tap your inner momentum to transform your business results.

*Empowered Women Inner Circle*
Where you can scale for impact and higher income.

*From Story to Profit Program*
Discover how to share a story allowing you to connect with your favourite coaching clients through 5 steps to articulate and monetise your message.

Details are available from anna-simpson.com/home or via scanning the QR code below.

www.ingramcontent.com/pod-product-compliance
Lightning Source LLC
Chambersburg PA
CBHW041308110526
44590CB00028B/4284